The 100

MOST IMPORTANT
New Yorkers

AGATHA EDWARDS

brooklyn bridge books

Brooklyn Bridge Books books may be purchased for educational, business, or sales promotional use. For information, please write us at Brooklynbridgebooks@gmail.com.

Edwards, Agatha (2003–)
  The 100 Most Important New Yorkers
  ISBN 978-0-692-90229-5

Cover and interior text design and layout
by Stephen Tiano, Book Designer
www.tianobookdesign.com

*This book is dedicated to those who believe
that anything in life is possible.
You can be born into the most humble of origins,
as so many in this book were,
and rise to become very important
to the lives of others.*

CONTENTS

Activists

1 Lillian Wald *Nurse and Activist* 15

2 Susan B. Anthony *Social Reformer and Activist* 16

3 Wong Chin Foo *Activist and Journalist* 17

4 Lewis Tappan *Abolitionist* 18

5 Rosetta "Mother" Gaston *Community Activist* 19

6 Samuel Gompers *Labor Union Leader* 20

7 Emma Goldman *Activist and Writer* 21

8 Victoria Earle Mathews *Activist and Writer* 22

9 Gershom Mendes Seixas *Jewish Community Leader* 23

10 Rose Schneiderman *Labor Organizer* 24

11 Jacob Riis *Social Reformer, Journalist, Photographer* 25

12 Josephine Shaw Lowell *Social Reformer* 26

13 Antonia Pantoja *Activist and Educator* 27

14 Mary White Ovington *Activist, Suffragette, Journalist* 28

Public Servants

15 Shirley Chisholm *Public Servant, Activist, Educator* 31

16 John Jay *Founding Father and Chief Justice* 32

17 Fiorello La Guardia *Public Servant* 33

18 Alexander Hamilton *Public Servant and Founding Father* 34

19 Ruth Bader Ginsburg *Supreme Court Justice* 35

20 Geraldine Ferraro *Public Servant* 36

21 Margaret Corbin *Revolutionary Soldier* 37

22 Rudy Giuliani *Public Servant and Entrepreneur* 38

23 Anne Hutchinson *Religious Leader and Colonizer* 39

24 Michael Bloomberg *Public Servant, Entrepreneur, Philanthropist* 40

25 Constance Baker Motley *Advocate and Jurist* 41

26 Felix Rohatyn *Public Servant and Financier* 42

27 Lady Deborah Moody *Colonizer and Religious Leader* 43

28 Franklin D. Roosevelt *Public Servant* 44

29 Eleanor Roosevelt *First Lady, Public Servant, Activist* 45

9

30   Theodore Roosevelt *Public Servant and Reformer*   46
31   Donald J. Trump *Public Servant and Entrepreneur*   47
32   Francis Perkins *Public Servant and Sociologist*   48
33   Mario Cuomo *Public Servant*   49
34   Henry Kissinger *Public Servant, Diplomat, Author*   50

Preservationists

35   Margot Gayle *Preservationist*   53
36   Jane Jacobs *Preservationist and Author*   54
37   Mathew Brady *Preservationist Photographer, Entrepreneur*   55
38   Jackie Kennedy Onassis *Preservationist, First Lady, Humanitarian*   56
39   Ruth Wittenburg *Preservationist*   57

Entrepreneurs

40   Dorothy Schiff *Newspaper Publisher*   61
41   Peter Cooper *Industrialist and Philanthropist*   62
42   Madame C.J. Walker *Entrepreneur and Activist*   63
43   Emily and Washington Roebling *Engineers and Bridge Builders*   64
44   George Steinbrenner *Baseball Owner*   65
45   Joseph "Joe" Papp *Theatre Producer*   66
46   Frederick Law Olmstead *Landscape Architect*   67
47   Fred Lebow *Sports Organizer*   68
48   Cornelius Vanderbilt *Entrepreneur*   69

Scientists and Explorers

49   Giovanni da Verrazzano *Explorer*   73
50   J. Robert Oppenheimer *Physicist*   74
51   Peter Minuit *Explorer and Administrator*   75
52   Robert Fulton *Inventor and Engineer*   76
53   David Ho *Scientist and Academic*   77
54   Peter Stuyvesant *Explorer and Public Servant*   78
55   Jonas Salk *Medical Researcher*   79
56   Susan McKinney-Steward *Doctor and Advocate*   80
57   Henry Hudson *Explorer*   81

CONTENTS

58   Carl Sagan *Astronomer and Educator*   *82*
59   Margaret Mead *Cultural Anthropologist*   *83*
60   Richard Feynman *Physicist and Writer*   *84*
61   Nikola Tesla *Inventor and Futurist*   *85*
62   Janet Yellen *Economist, Educator, Public Servant*   *86*

Philanthropists

63   Brook Astor *Philanthropist and Writer*   *89*
64   Pierre Toussaint *Philanthropist*   *90*
65   Abby Aldrich Rockefeller *Philanthropist*   *91*
66   Peggy Guggenheim *Philanthropist and Arts Patron*   *92*
67   Alfred T. White *Philanthropist and Social Reformer*   *93*

Artists

68   Andy Warhol *Artist*   *97*
69   Langston Hughes *Poet, Playwright, Cultural Leader*   *98*
70   Agnes de Mille *Choreographer and Dancer*   *99*
71   Jerry Seinfield *Comedian, Actor, Producer*   *100*
72   Alice Austen *Photographer*   *101*
73   Jim Henson *Puppeteer and Artist*   *102*
74   Louis Comfort Tiffany *Artist and Entrepreneur*   *103*
75   Ralph Ellison *Novelist, Essayist, Scholar*   *104*
76   Martin Scorsese *Film Director, Producer, Actor*   *105*
77   Martha Graham *Choreographer and Dancer*   *106*
78   Eugene O'Neill *Playwright*   *107*
79   Billie Holiday *Singer*   *108*
80   The Marx Brothers *Entertainers*   *109*
81   James Baldwin *Novelist and Activist*   *110*
82   Margaret Bourke-White *Photographer*   *111*
83   George Balanchine *Choreographer*   *112*
84   George Gershwin *Composer and Pianist*   *113*

Writers and Journalists

85   Nellie Bly *Writer and Entrepreneur*   *117*

86   Zora Neale Hurston *Writer and Folklorist*   *118*

87   **Jimmy Breslin** *Reporter*   *119*

88   Ada Louise Huxtable *Writer and Architectural Critic*   *120*

89   **Walt Whitman** *Poet and Humanist*   *121*

90   **Dorothy Parker** *Writer and Satirist*   *122*

91   **Ayn Rand** *Writer and Philosopher*   *123*

92   **Isaac Asimov** *Writer and Futurist*   *124*

Sports Figures

93   **Jackie Robinson** *Baseball Player*   *127*

94   **George Herman "Babe" Ruth** *Baseball Player*   *128*

95   **Vince Lombardi** *Football Coach*   *129*

96   **Althea Gibson** *Tennis and Golf Player*   *130*

97   **Joe DiMaggio** *Baseball Player*   *131*

98   **Joe "Willie" Namath** *Football Player*   *132*

99   **Arthur Ashe** *Tennis Player and Humanitarian*   *133*

100 Kareem Abdul-Jabbar *Basketball Player and Humanitarian*   *134*

YOU MIGHT ALSO CONSIDER   *135*

PHOTO CREDITS   *137*

ACKNOWLEDGMENTS   *143*

INDEX   *145*

Activists

LILLIAN WALD

BORN: 3/10/1867
DIED: 9/1/1940
OCCUPATION: Nurse and Activist

Her life was completely devoted to helping others. Born into a middle-class German-Jewish family in Cincinnati, Ms. Wald moved to New York for nursing school and graduated in 1891. She was so shaken by the conditions in tenements that she had to make changes. In 1893 she opened the Visiting Nurse Service for the poor. In 1895 she began the Henry Street Settlement. Women and the poor remained her priority so she helped found the Women's Trade Union League in 1903 and the Children's Bureau in 1912. She co-founded Lincoln House to provide health care to black New Yorkers, and in 1909 she assisted in founding the NAACP. As WWI began, she joined the Woman's Peace Party and led 1,000 New York women to protest the war in 1914. She founded the Henry Street Neighborhood Playhouse in 1915. That year she was also elected president of a new organization: The American Union Against Militarism. In the 1920s she attempted to amend the U.S. constitution to ban child labor. After she died in 1940, a tribute was held at Carnegie Hall and 2,000 people showed up.

BIO BITS

• She first used the name 'public health nurse' for nurses serving the public.
• *The New York Times* named her one of the 12 greatest American women in 1922.
• She never married.

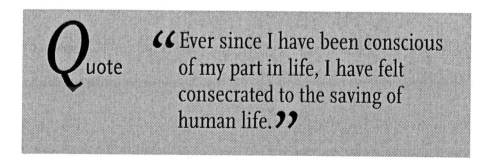

*Q*uote **" Ever since I have been conscious of my part in life, I have felt consecrated to the saving of human life. "**

2

SUSAN B. ANTHONY
BORN: 2/15/1820
DIED: 3/13/1906
OCCUPATION: Social Reformer and Activist

Even at 17 she was already an activist—and that left 70 more years for her to work for social justice. She started by collecting petitions against slavery in 1837 at the age of 17. On she worked and in 1856 she was named New York's state agent for the American Anti-Slavery Society. With her friend Elizabeth Cady Stanton, she founded the New York Women's State Temperance Society (to stop alcoholic drinking) in 1852. In 1866 they initiated the American Equal Rights Association to fight for equal rights for women and African Americans. In 1869 they founded the National Woman Suffrage Association (for a woman's right to vote). In 1872 Anthony was arrested for voting in Rochester, New York. She was convicted but never paid a fine and they left her alone. She gave 75 to 100 speeches each year for women's suffrage. Though she and Stanton gave Congress an amendment for the woman's vote in 1878 (known as the Anthony Amendment), it took until 1920 for the Nineteenth Amendment to pass, which was 14 years after her death.

BIO BITS
- She was raised a devout Quaker and was schooled in Philadelphia for a time.
- Her family farm was a meeting place for abolitionists, including Frederick Douglass.
- She was the first woman put on U.S. money: the dollar coin in 1979.

*Q*uote **❝Men, their rights and nothing more; women, their rights and nothing less.❞**

WONG CHIN FOO
BORN: 1847
DIED: 1898
OCCUPATION: Activist and Journalist

He was the first person known to use the phrase *Chinese American* and is considered their Dr. Martin Luther King. He was born in Shandong Province to a well-off family that lost its fortune during the Taiping Rebellion. A missionary took him in as a Baptist and brought him to the U.S. in 1867. He studied here and widely traveled. He returned to China in 1870, worked, then barely escaped arrest for attempting to overthrow a corrupt government. He returned to the U.S. and became a citizen in 1874. He fought Chinese discrimination, lectured extensively and settled in NYC in 1883. He started a paper, *The Chinese American*: the first known time that phrase was used. He wrote for *The Brooklyn Eagle* and his pieces about Chinese life were widely published around the country. He brought a Chinese theatre to NYC, established a language school and opened a Confucian temple. He founded the county's first association of Chinese American voters, as well as the Chinese Equal Rights League in 1892. He testified before Congress to support Chinese rights and inclusion.

BIO BITS
- The missionary who took him in at age 20 was murdered soon afterward.
- He opened a tea shop in Bay City, Michigan in 1880.
- He introduced Americans to "chop suey" in an article for the *Brooklyn Eagle*.

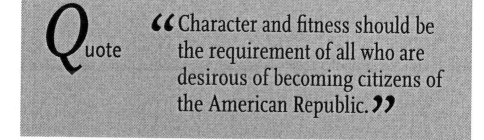

*Q*uote **"Character and fitness should be the requirement of all who are desirous of becoming citizens of the American Republic."**

LEWIS TAPPAN
BORN: 5/23/1788
DIED: 6/21/1873
OCCUPATION: Abolitionist

He and his Massachusetts-born brother, Arthur, were among America's strongest abolitionists. From a religious family, he came to NYC in 1826 to begin a silk importing business, but saving souls was his true mission. He started own newspaper, which prohibited immoral ads. He infuriated anti-abolitionists so much that in 1834 his business was attacked and a mob rampaged his home and burned his furniture in the street. Slave holders offered a $100,000 reward if anyone could kill the Tappan brothers and bring their dead bodies to a slave state. 1839 brought the Amistad case. He provided money to defend the African mutineers and recruited John Quincy Adams as their lawyer. He arranged for tutoring the captives in English. His money was poured into progressive causes: abolition, temperance, and the creation of Oberlin College to provided an integrated education. He helped found the American and Foreign Anti-Slavery Society, which called for equal rights for African Americans, and he donated money to the Underground Railroad before and during the Civil War.

BIO BITS

- He advocated intermarriage to solve America's racial issues.
- He worked closely with Frederick Douglass and Samuel Cornish.
- He voted for Republican Abraham Lincoln in 1860 and 1864.

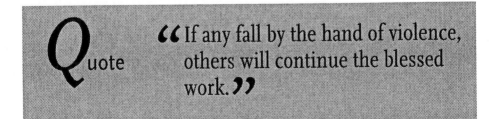

*Q*uote **" If any fall by the hand of violence, others will continue the blessed work. "**

ROSETTA "MOTHER" GASTON
BORN: 1885
DIED: February, 1981
OCCUPATION: Community Leader and Educator

Though less then five feet tall, she was a community giant. Born in a tenement in 1885, she left school to support her family, eventually taking a job running an elevator at Bergdorf Goodman on 5th Avenue and 57th—for 40 years. But her life's work was in her Brownsville neighborhood where she sponsored heritage studies. She met Carter G. Woodson in 1943. He encouraged her to open a chapter of the Association for Study of Negro Life and History. She did, assisted by donations from Bergdorf's. For decades she organized history lessons for African-Americans. She made a Children's Cultural Corner inside her own apartment in 1969 where she taught. She got the name "Mother" because she was like a mother to so many children. Her dream was the formation of a site where the community could come to learn about their heritage. After 50 years of dreaming, that was achieved a month after she died when Heritage House, which she founded, opened on the 2nd floor of the Stone Avenue Branch of the Brooklyn Public Library in Brownsville.

BIO BITS
- Stone Avenue was renamed Mother Gaston Boulevard and a statue placed nearby.
- When children trick-or-treated, she gave pennies and bits of African-American history for Halloween.
- She became close friends with Carter G. Woodson and Mary McLeod Bethune.

Quote **"** I wanted to empower the youth and make them proud of their common heritage ... This idea was the seed for the Heritage House. **"**

SAMUEL GOMPERS
BORN: 1/27/1850
DIED: 12/13/1924
OCCUPATION: Labor Union Leader

At age 10 he was pulled out of his Jewish school in London to make cigars, an event having a lifelong impact. Due to poverty, his family immigrated to Houston Street on the Lower East Side in 1863. His dad made cigars at home, then Gompers was soon working in cigar shops. He became president of the Cigarmakers International Union in 1875 to help workers fight for rights. In 1886 he became president of the American Federation of Labor (AFL) which had 50,000 members; by the time of his death in 1924, the AFL had over 3 million members. He brought workers together with a goal of obtaining fair wages, reasonable working hours, and mutual aid in dire times. He built the labor movement into a force that heightened workers' power. He called a nationwide strike in 1886 to support the 8-hour workday. He was a strong supporter of WWI and President Wilson appointed him to the Council of National Defense. He traveled widely for labor throughout North America and the world. His efforts transformed the rights of workers throughout the U.S.

BIO BITS

- He had 12 children but only 6 survived infancy.
- He is buried in the Sleepy Hollow Cemetery in New York.
- He learned to speak German while working at benches rolling cigars alongside German workers.

*Q*uote **"**The man who has his millions will want everything he can lay his hands on and then raise his voice against the poor devil who wants ten cents more a day.**"**

EMMA GOLDMAN

BORN: 6/27/1869
DIED: 5/14/1940
OCCUPATION: Activist and Writer

She was the greatest anarchist in America. Born into an Orthodox Jewish family in Lithuania, she was violently punished by her father. He tried to force her to marry at 15. She wouldn't. He let her come to America at 16, then she worked sewing clothes 10 hours-a-day for $2.50 a week. She moved to NYC with $5 and a sewing machine. She met radicals and became a famous anarchist orator. She barely escaped jail for plotting to assassinate Henry Clay Frick, but the evidence could not put her on trial. She was jailed a year for "inciting a riot." She was implicated in President McKinley's death but not tried. She became a nurse. She started a magazine called *Mother Earth* in 1906 with a radical philosophy. She orated widely for socialism and birth control. She opposed conscription for WWI, was jailed 2 years for it, then deported from the U.S. She went to Russia to support the Bolsheviks but left upon seeing it was a sham. She went to Spain for that Civil War in 1936, then to England, then Canada, opposing fascists to her end.

BIO BITS

- She wrote 6 books, including an autobiography, and countless articles.
- While alive, she was regarded as "the most dangerous woman in America."
- She is buried near Chicago in the Forest Home Cemetery with other radicals.

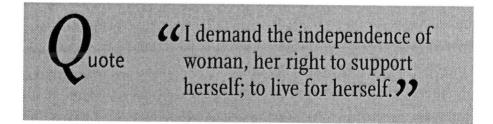

Quote **"I demand the independence of woman, her right to support herself; to live for herself."**

VICTORIA EARLE MATHEWS
BORN: 5/27/1861
DIED: 3/10/1907
OCCUPATION: Activist and Writer

She rose from slavery to help countless New Yorkers. Born in Georgia during the Civil War (her father was a slaveholder so she was half-white), at age eight she was taken to NYC. She attended public school but left to support her family as a servant. The house where she worked had a library; the owner saw her trying to read so he let her freely use books when her chores were finished. She read often and turned herself into a journalist and fiction writer. She helped found the *Woman's Loyal Union*, which fought lynching and discrimination. In 1896 she became chairwoman of the *National Association of Colored Women*. She was highly sought to speak on racial pride and self-esteem. She helped purchased a house at 217 E. 86th, which became the White Rose Home for Working Class Negro Girls. She taught families during the Great Migration how to prepare meals, sew, do laundry and find work. She especially sought safe quarters for abused women and victims of violence. She was one of the nation's most respected African Americans at the time of her death.

BIO BITS
- She published a book in 1893 titled *Aunt Lindy.*
- She became a Salvation Army field officer and missionary.
- She is buried in Maple Grove Cemetery in Queens and her tombstone reads: She Hath Done What She Could.

Quote **"Let women and girls become enlightened, let them begin to think."**

GERSHOM MENDES SEIXAS
BORN: 1/15/1746
DIED: 7/2/1816
OCCUPATION: Jewish Community Leader

He is considered the first true American Jewish leader. His father fled religious tyranny in Portugal and arrived in NYC in 1730, then he married in 1741. In the 1760s, NYC had fewer than 300 Jews and a single synagogue. At age 23, in 1768, Seixas was appointed *Hazzan* (no rabbis were present). Seixas performed marriages and funerals and took over the duties ascribed to rabbis. He was self-educated in Talmud and religious texts. He strongly supported the Revolution against England (called the 'Patriot Preacher') and asked his congregation to bless the Congress and George Washington. He fled to Philadelphia when the British overtook NYC, then later returned. He was a friend to all and Christians selected him in 1784 to be a trustee of Columbia College. He devoted his time to acts of charity for the poor. He was so esteemed that when George Washington was inaugurated in NYC in 1789, he was one of 14 ministers invited to participate. The trustees of Columbia College commissioned a medal to him as an honor upon his death.

BIO BITS
- One of his brothers fought in the Continental Army and another helped form the NY Stock Exchange.
- His son, David, established the Pennsylvania Institution for the Deaf and Dumb.
- He is interred in the First Shearith Israel Graveyard near Chatham Square in NYC.

*Q*uote **" May the Lord our God be with us, as he was with our fathers. "**

10

ROSE SCHNEIDERMAN
BORN: 4/6/1882
DIED: 8/11/1972
OCCUPATION: Labor Organizer

She was born in Poland into a poor Jewish family. At age 8 they immigrated to the Lower East Side, but two years later her father died, leaving the family in poverty. Her mother sewed for money but, for a while, she and her three siblings lived in an orphanage. She left school at 11 to work as a cashier, then to sew caps. She became involved in unions and helped start a union in her factory in 1903. She rose to leadership positions and led a massive strike of 20,000 workers in 1909. After the Triangle Shirtwaist Factory fire of 1911, where 146 workers burned alive or jumped to their deaths, she sought protections for workers, then became the national president of the Women's Trade Union League. She fought for Women's Suffrage and helped NY State give women the right to vote in 1917. She was a founding member of the ACLU and worked for President Roosevelt during the Great Depression. She advised Eleanor and Franklin Roosevelt on labor matters and was their friend. From 1937–44, she was Secretary of Labor for NY State. She died in NYC at age 90.

BIO BITS
- Her mother had to feed the family from charity food baskets on the LES.
- She worked hard in the 1930s–40s to resettle European Jews in the U.S. and Palestine.
- She never married but had a long-term partner in colleague Maud Swartz.

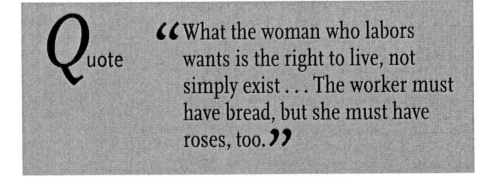

Quote

“What the woman who labors wants is the right to live, not simply exist . . . The worker must have bread, but she must have roses, too.”

JACOB RIIS
BORN: 5/3/1849
DIED: 5/26/1914
OCCUPATION: Social Reformer, Journalist, Photographer

He began as a police reporter and ended up affecting countless lives. He was born and grew up in Denmark, intending to be a carpenter. But when there was little employment, at age 21, he immigrated to the U.S. He went through an incredible variety of jobs and was destitute for a long period. He eventually landed a job as a reporter and editor. He returned to Denmark to marry the girl of his dreams and they returned to New York. Riis got a job as a police reporter and his beat was the worst slum in NYC. He decided he would try to change the slums through journalism. He photographed them to show the penury and documented the hardships of the poor. He wrote in magazines and published books. He became friends with Teddy Roosevelt, who called him, "The best American I ever knew." His reports on city water pollution led the government to purchase the Croton Reservoir and protect citizens from cholera. He was responsible for instigating a park program around the worst tenements and advocated that the rich devote philanthropy to social programs.

BIO BITS
- He met the girl who would become his wife when he was 16 and she was 12.
- He was briefly editor of the *Brooklyn News*, which is still published.
- His first wife died in 1905; he remarried in 1907. His second wife lived until 1967.

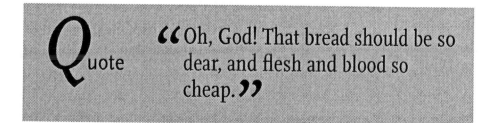

Quote   **❝** Oh, God! That bread should be so dear, and flesh and blood so cheap. **❞**

JOSEPHINE SHAW LOWELL

BORN: 12/16/1843
DIED: 10/12/1905
OCCUPATION: Social Reformer

Born to intellectual parents, her family set-tled on Staten Island while she was a child. In 1863 she married and followed her husband to Virginia while he served in the Civil War. She became a nurse to the wounded in battle. Then her husband was killed in 1864, a month before her baby was born. She returned to Staten Island to live with her parents and became a Progressive. She was active in the Anti-Imperialist League and supported Philippine independence. She hoped to eradicate poverty and worked for social justice. In 1876 she was the first woman appointed Commissioner of NY State Board of Charities. She founded many organizations: the NY Charity Organization in 1882; the House of Refuge for Women in 1886; the Woman's Municipal League in 1894; and the Civil Service Reform Association in 1895. Most significantly, she established the NY Consumer's League in 1890 to improve wages and working conditions for women in New York. The League expanded to branches around the country and fights to this day for consumer and worker rights.

BIO BITS
- Her mother was considered to be the "genius" of the family.
- Her brother also died in the Civil War while leading the first black Union Regiment.
- She never remarried and always dressed in black.

Quote

"If it could only be drummed into the rich that what the poor want is fair wages and not little doles of food, we should not have all this suffering and misery and vice."

ANTONIA PANTOJA

BORN: 9/13/1922
DIED: 5/24/2002
OCCUPATION: Activist and Educator

She saw discrimination against Latinos and set out to change it. Born in Puerto Rico, she lived there until 22, then moved to NYC, taking a job as a factory welder. Recognizing the lack of power and knowledge for Puerto Ricans, she became an activist to help repair the community. In 1952 she completed a bachelor's degree from Hunter College. She then went to Columbia for her master's in social work in 1954. In 1957 she founded the Puerto Rico Forum with a goal of promoting economic self-sufficiency. She founded ASPIRA (Spanish for aspire) in 1961 to help Latinos achieve their dreams through education and community. Serving more than 85,000 students each year, ASPIRA provides educational counseling and financial assistance. Then she helped form the Puerto Rican Community Development Project. She established Boricua College in NYC in 1970, now with three campuses. In Washington, D.C., she formed the Puerto Rican Research and Resources Center. She completed her Ph.D. in 1973 and assisted Latino organizations throughout the country.

BIO BITS

- She was the first Puerto Rican woman to receive the Presidential Medal of Freedom in 1966.
- She founded a graduate school at San Diego State University.
- She came out as LGBT in 2002 with her autobiography, *Memoir of a Visionary*.

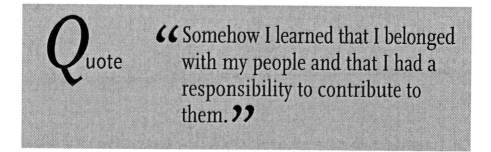

*Q*uote **❝** Somehow I learned that I belonged with my people and that I had a responsibility to contribute to them. **❞**

MARY WHITE OVINGTON
BORN: 4/11/1865
DIED: 7/15/1951
OCCUPATION: Activist, Suffragette and Journalist

Her life was devoted to helping the poor and advancing the well-being of African Americans. Born in Brooklyn three days after Lincoln was shot, she was educated at Packer Institute and the Harvard Annex. She worked at Pratt Institute, then the Greenpoint Settlement, improving conditions for the indigent. She heard Booker T. Washington speak and it profoundly affected her. She corresponded with W. E. B. Dubois. She worked to aid settlement communities in Manhattan and Brooklyn. She helped organize a mixed-race conference in 1910 to advance the interest of the Negro. It evolved into the NAACP: National Association for the Advancement of Colored People. Participating were blacks, whites, scholars and clergy—all with the goal of improving conditions for African Americans. She served with the NAACP from 1910 to 1947 and was always on the Executive Board. She raised money, held conferences, and marketed the NAACP. She was also a fighter for women's suffrage.

BIO BITS
- She wrote three novels and children's books, including 1911's, *Half a Man*.
- Her church was the Second Unitarian Church in Cobble Hill, demolished in 1962.
- PS/IS 30 in Brooklyn on 4th Avenue was recently built and named for her.

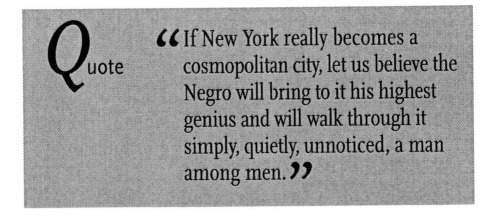

*Q*uote **❝** If New York really becomes a cosmopolitan city, let us believe the Negro will bring to it his highest genius and will walk through it simply, quietly, unnoticed, a man among men. **❞**

Public Servants

SHIRLEY CHISHOLM
BORN: 11/30/1924
DIED: 1/1/2005
OCCUPATION: Public Servant, Activist and Educator

She was the first African American to run for president from a major party: the Democrats. Chisholm was born in Brooklyn but spent part of her childhood in Barbados with her grandmother, which gave her a lifelong West Indian accent. Her father was a baker and also made burlap bags; her mother was a domestic worker. She graduated from Brooklyn College in 1946, then became a teacher and received a master's degree from Columbia University. After working for NYC's child welfare programs, Chisholm ran for congress in 1968. She won and was the first African-American congresswoman. She served seven terms and was a huge advocate for children and the poor. In 1969 she became a founding member of the Congressional Black Caucus. In 1972 she had a fiery run for president, but lost. One of her legislative successes was getting unemployment benefits extended to domestic workers. She later taught at Mount Holyoke College and toured the country speaking for children's and human rights. In 2015, she was awarded the Presidential Medal of Freedom.

BIO BITS
- She attended the famous Girls' High School in Bed-Stuy, Brooklyn.
- From 1953–59 she ran children's nurseries in Brownsville and Manhattan.
- She wrote two autobiographies, one titled: *Unbought and Unbossed*.

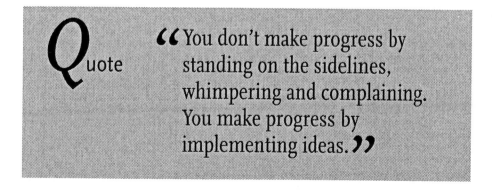

*Q*uote **"** You don't make progress by standing on the sidelines, whimpering and complaining. You make progress by implementing ideas. **"**

JOHN JAY

BORN: 12/23/1745
DIED: 5/17/1829
OCCUPATION: Founding Father and Chief Justice

He tried to end slavery in New York in 1777 and stayed at it until he succeeded in 1799. Born in NYC, he was one of 10 children from a wealthy family. He attended King's College (now Columbia University) in 1760. He became a lawyer and tried to protect American rights while the British imposed strict rule. He was a moderate, then became a staunch patriot for independence. During the Revolutionary War, he was a delegate for both Continental Congresses. Jay fiercely opposed slavery and founded a boycott of newspapers and merchants involved in the slave trade. He was the new nation's Secretary for Foreign Affairs from 1784–89. Importantly, he wrote five of the Federalist Papers, advocating that the U.S. have a strong but balanced government. In 1789, George Washington offered him the position of first Chief Justice, which he accepted. Under Jay's leadership, the Supreme Court established the procedures for our current court system. He then took the job of New York governor from 1795–1801 and it was then that the state ended slavery.

BIO BITS

- Two of his siblings contracted smallpox and were blinded for life; he supported them for the rest of their lives.
- He was 28-years-old when he married his wife, who was 17.
- John Jay College of Criminal Justice opened for its first class in 1965.

Quote **❝No power on earth has a right to take our property from us without consent.❞**

FIORELLO La GUARDIA
BORN: 12/11/1882
DIED: 9/20/1947
OCCUPATION: Public Servant

He is considered one of America's best mayors ever. His father was a southern Italian Catholic, his mother a northern Italian Jew. He was born in Greenwich Village. After graduating from school, he worked for the State Department overseas, then returned for a law degree at NYU. He was an interpreter at Ellis Island from 1907–1910. He was elected to the House of Representatives in 1916 but had to leave it to fight overseas in WWI. La Guardia returned to Congress from 1922–1933 and was a tireless champion for progressive causes and immigrants. He won a tight race for mayor in 1933, then had many accomplishments: he fought mob corruption; shut down the Tammany Hall machine; supported Franklin Roosevelt, though FDR was a Democrat and he a Republican; restored faith in City Hall; built low-cost public housing, parks and airports; reorganized the police force; and he awarded jobs on the basis of merit rather than patronage. He was a constant champion for New York's ethnic minorities who loved him for his endurance, toughness and humor.

BIO BITS
- He was only 5'2" tall and his nickname was, "The Little Flower."
- He reportedly spoke English, Hebrew, Italian, German, Croatian and Yiddish.
- A performing arts high school beside Lincoln Center is named after him.

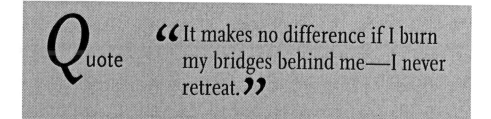

Quote *"It makes no difference if I burn my bridges behind me—I never retreat."*

ALEXANDER HAMILTON

BORN: 1/11/1757
DIED: 7/12/1804
OCCUPATION: Public Servant and Founding Father

Pick up a ten-dollar bill and look in the eyes of a great New Yorker. This Founding Father wasn't born here, he was born on an island off Puerto Rico. His own father was a Scot, his mother of French descent, and he was conceived out-of-wedlock. He was a very intelligent boy so his aunts saved money to send him to school in New Jersey at age 16. After that he helped fight the British in the Revolutionary War. George Washington made Hamilton his special aide upon seeing his insightful thinking. Post-independence, Hamilton assisted in writing the Federalist Papers. He was appointed our first Secretary of the Treasury when America had to find a way to pay for the new government. Hamilton helped elect Thomas Jefferson president when the vote was tied between Jefferson and Aaron Burr. In 1804, Burr was so angered by Hamilton's writings that he challenged him to a duel with pistols. Hamilton was shot in New Jersey, then ferried to Greenwich Village, where he died at 80–82 Jane Street. He is buried in Trinity Churchyard Cemetery in Manhattan.

BIO BITS
- He personally led an attack against the British at the Battle of Yorktown.
- He studied for exams on his own and became a lawyer in just six months.
- He founded *The New York Post* in 1801, though its original name was *The New York Evening Post*.

> Quote
> **"People sometimes attribute my success to my genius; all the genius I know anything about is hard work."**

RUTH BADER GINSBURG

BORN: 3/15/1933
DIED: —
OCCUPATION: Supreme Court Justice

Her parents were Russian Jewish immigrants who lived in the Flatbush section of Brooklyn; she became the Notorious RBG. Her mother was forced to leave school and work at age 15 and wanted a great education for her daughter, so she often took Ruth to libraries. She attended James Madison High School (her mother died of cancer the day before her high school graduation). Ginsburg went on to Cornell University and there met her future husband at age 17. She married him a month after graduation. She went to Harvard Law School as one of only nine women admitted to a class of 500. She then transferred to Columbia (finishing first in her class) when her husband got a job in NYC. Being a woman made it hard to get work because men were preferred as lawyers. She got a job at Rutgers, then with the ACLU, where she took many cases concerning gender discrimination. President Carter appointed her to the U.S. Court of Appeals in 1980, and Bill Clinton nominated her for the Supreme Court in 1993 as the second female Justice. She is widely celebrated for her generous wit and tremendous intelligence.

BIO BITS

- Though a liberal, she was great friends with conservative Justice Antonin Scalia.
- Her book, *My Own Words*, was a *New York Times* bestseller.
- Her son, James, is founder of Cedille Records, a classical recording label.

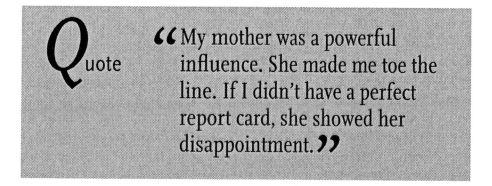

*Q*uote **❝My mother was a powerful influence. She made me toe the line. If I didn't have a perfect report card, she showed her disappointment.❞**

GERALDINE FERRARO
BORN: 8/26/1935
DIED: 3/26/2011
OCCUPATION: Public Servant

She was a public school teacher who went on to be the first female vice-presidential candidate. She attended Catholic schools. Her father, an Italian immigrant, died of a heart attack when she was only eight. Her mother was forced to move to a low-income area in South Bronx. Ferraro was smart and got a scholarship to Marymount Manhattan College, working at the same time. She was the first in her family to get a college degree. She worked as a teacher in Astoria but wanted to attend law school so went to Fordham at night while teaching second grade. In 1974 she became Assistant District Attorney for Queens and was a strong advocate for abused children. In 1978 she won the race for U.S. Representative and gained the respect of other politicians for her tough-but-fair attitude. In 1984 Walter Mondale was the Democratic candidate for president and selected her as his running mate. American women were thrilled and Ferraro gave an inspiring acceptance speech. The team lost to Ronald Reagan but history was made and a glass ceiling shattered.

BIO BITS
- Her autobiography, *Ferraro: My Story*, earned her over $1 million.
- In 1993 she became the U.S. ambassador to the U.N. for Human Rights.
- She is buried in St. John's Cemetery in her old congressional district in Queens.

*Q*uote **"We've chosen the path to equality, don't let them turn us around."**

MARGARET CORBIN
BORN: 11/12/1751
DIED: 1/16/1800
OCCUPATION: Revolutionary Soldier

At age five her father was killed in an Indian raid and her mother captured, never to be seen again. Corbin was then raised by an uncle. She married a man in the Pennsylvania militia in 1772 so followed Revolutionary soldiers around in camps while doing tasks like cooking, laundry, and caring for the wounded. During battles she would run water back and forth to thirsty soldiers, which was also used in cooling cannons. In 1776 she dressed like a man and joined in the Battle of Fort Washington in northern Manhattan. It was 600 American patriots against 4,000 enemy troops. Her husband was killed in battle, then she took his place, firing his cannon against the British. She was wounded in the arm, chest and jaw but bravely kept fighting until she was captured. The enemy then gave her back to a Revolutionary hospital but she had lost the use of her left arm for the rest of her life. She went on to West Point to care for wounded soldiers. Later she was the first woman given a military pension by the U.S. Congress for her courageous service.

BIO BITS

- A memorial was erected to her in 1909 that stands in Fort Tryon Park.
- In 1926 she was given full military honors and her remains moved to West Point.
- She remarried but her second husband died a year later.

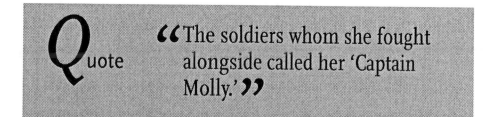

Quote **"The soldiers whom she fought alongside called her 'Captain Molly.'"**

RUDY GIULIANI

BORN: 5/28/1944
DIED: —
OCCUPATION: Public Servant and Entrepreneur

His nickname: "America's Mayor." The grandson of Italian immigrants and born in the East Flatbush section of Brooklyn, Giulani had a blue-collar upbringing. His dad was a plumber and bartender. He was educated in Catholic schools and considered being a priest. After college he became a law clerk and a U.S. Attorney. He was elected mayor in 1993 and quickly sought to reduce crime. He used a policy called "broken windows" where the police enforced even the smallest infraction. It worked and in two years he reduced police shootings by one-third and cut NYC's murder rate in half. He also instituted a successful "welfare-to-work" program that led 600,000 poor New Yorkers to leave governmental dependency for private employment. His biggest challenge came in 2001 when Al-Qaeda flew two jets into the World Trade Center. It was devastating to New York as more than 2,700 people were killed and more suffered severe medical problems. It is said that his heroic leadership saved 20,000 people and he rallied the city and country at one of our nation's lowest points.

BIO BITS

- He was *Time* Magazine's Person of the Year in 2001.
- He voted for Democrat George McGovern in 1972.
- He lost his first race for mayor against David Dinkins in 1989 by 47,080 votes.

Quote **"**Tomorrow New York is going to be here. And we're going to rebuild, and we're going to be stronger than we were before.**"**

ANNE HUTCHINSON
BORN: 7/20/1591
DIED: c. August, 1643
OCCUPATION: Religious Leader and Colonizer

She almost destroyed the Puritan colony of New England then ended up a hero for religious freedom. Born in England, she moved to Boston in 1633 with 11 children (she had four more). She was a midwife. She adopted a religion based on 'grace' rather than 'works.' When she tried to convert other Puritans, she was tried and banished from the Massachusetts Colony. She traveled by foot for six days through the snow to reach Rhode Island. After four years there, the Boston Puritans threatened to claim that colony so she had to move again. Now she traveled to land that was not controlled by the English but land the Dutch held: New Netherland. It was in north Bronx, near the Hutchinson River. She arrived with 7 children and 16 total people in her group. One year later, disaster struck. She and her family were massacred by Indians except for one daughter who was out picking blueberries. That daughter (Susanna) was captured by Indians and renamed Autumn Leaf. She was held for two years then ransomed back to family members living in Boston.

BIO BITS
- The Hutchinson River Parkway is named after her.
- Her descendents include Franklin Roosevelt and the Bush family.
- She died when she was scalped by Indians.

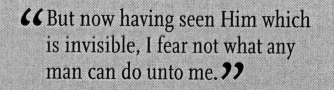

*Q*uote **"**But now having seen Him which is invisible, I fear not what any man can do unto me.**"**

MICHAEL BLOOMBERG
BORN: 2/14/1942
DIED: —
OCCUPATION: Public Servant and Philanthropist

He is a self-made man who has made life much better for millions of others. Born in Boston, his father was a bookkeeper for a dairy company. Bloomberg had to put himself through college. After completing a master's at Harvard, he took a job on Wall Street in 1966 and rose quickly. In 1981 he started a company that used computers to process financial information. His computer terminals were adopted everywhere and his company made billions of dollars. That turned him into one of the richest men in the world. His business expanded into other media, radio and television. In 2001 he was elected mayor of New York as a liberal Republican. He established the 311 telephone line for NYC and revamped the education system. He brought non-partisan decision-making to the job. He served 12 years and is considered the most practical mayor in NYC history. He is a devoted environmentalist who continuously fights climate change and is a staunch supporter of gun control. He has given billions in contributions to charities to support New Yorkers in all fields.

BIO BITS
- He was an Eagle Scout.
- His undergraduate degree was in electrical engineering from Johns Hopkins.
- In 2015 he was America's third largest philanthropic donor.

Quote **"This is the city of dreamers and time and again it's the place where the greatest dream of all, the American dream, has been tested and has triumphed."**

CONSTANCE BAKER MOTLEY
BORN: 9/14/1921
DIED: 9/28/2005
OCCUPATION: Advocate and Jurist

She argued many of the countries greatest cases before the Supreme Court. Born in New Haven, CT to Caribbean immigrants, she was the 9th of 12 children. Her mother was a maid and her father a chef at Yale. She went to public schools, attended NYU and graduated in 1943. She received a law degree from Columbia in 1946. Supreme Court Justice Thurgood Marshall hired her as a clerk. After that she worked for the NAACP, visiting Dr. Martin Luther King in jail and Medgar Evers while under armed guard. She wrote the original complaint in *Brown v. Board of Education*. She was the first African-American woman to argue before the Supreme Court in *Meredith v. Fair*. She won 9 of 10 cases before the Supreme Court—her one loss was later overturned in her favor. When James Meredith appealed to be the first black student at the University of Mississippi in 1962, she won the case. Her legal efforts helped desegregate the South. She served in the State Senate, was Manhattan Borough President and was appointed the first African-American federal judge.

BIO BITS
- She was the first African-American woman accepted into Columbia Law School.
- She was the first woman elected to the New York State Senate in 1964.
- In 1978 she ruled that a female reporter must be allowed into the Yankees locker room.

Quote

"When I was 15, I decided I wanted to be a lawyer. No one thought this was a good idea."

FELIX ROHATYN
BORN: 5/29/1928
DIED: —
OCCUPATION: Public Servant and Financier

Born a Polish Jew in Austria before WWII, he later helped save NYC from bankruptcy. His family fled the Germans before WWII, then went to Casablanca, then to Brazil, and finally landed in NYC in 1942. He went to the YMCA's McBurney School on 63rd Street. He served in the Army during the Korean War. After that, Rohatyn got a Wall Street finance job and did very well. In 1975 the city ran out of money and was on the verge of bankruptcy because of huge expenses and debts. If that occurred, policemen, firefighters, garbage men, and millions of city employees would have no paycheck. Governor Carey appointed Rohatyn to solve the problem. He led a group that forced New York to make layoffs and imposed wage freezes. He also raised the subway fare and charged tuition at City University. Rohatyn worked with banks to hold off bankruptcy long enough for the city to return to financial health. It was a difficult time because the city payroll was cut by 40,000 and daycare centers had to close, but his measures worked and New York was back in business.

BIO BITS
- His great-grandfather was Grand Rabbi of Poland.
- President Clinton appointed him Ambassador to France.
- During the Korean War he served in the rank of sergeant.

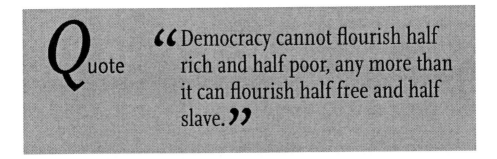

Quote **"Democracy cannot flourish half rich and half poor, any more than it can flourish half free and half slave."**

27

LADY DEBORAH MOODY
BORN: 1586
DIED: 1659
OCCUPATION: Colonizer and Religious Leader

She was the first female landowner in the New World and one leader described her as "a dangerous woman." Moody was born in London, the daughter of a bishop. She grew up at a time when Shakespeare's plays were performed. She married but her husband died in 1629, then she converted to the religion called *Anabaptist*. She was persecuted for that so, at age 54 in 1639, she left for the New World and religious freedom. She settled in Massachusetts but was scorned by the Puritans and banished. Moody led a group of dissenters to Dutch territory in New Netherland and there she founded the town of Gravesend, which is now part of Brooklyn. Peter Stuyvesant gave her 7,000 acres of land for her colony. Her followers ran into trouble with Indians and were attacked, but survived. Then they were scorned by other colonies around them for their beliefs. But neither Moody, nor the people of Gravesend, bent to the religious will of others. She let her people worship as they pleased. She was the power behind her colony until her death at age 73.

BIO BITS
- Some of the streets she laid out in Gravesend in 1643 are still there today.
- She is believed to be buried in Old Gravesend Cemetery in an unmarked grave.
- P.S. 212 Lady Deborah Moody School on Bay 49th street is named for her.

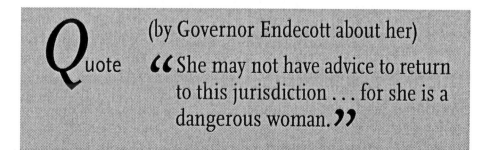

Quote (by Governor Endecott about her) **"**She may not have advice to return to this jurisdiction . . . for she is a dangerous woman.**"**

28

FRANKLIN D. ROOSEVELT
BORN: 1/30/1882
DIED: 4/12/1945
OCCUPATION: Public Servant

He served as president for 13 years during the most traumatic events of the 20th Century: the Great Depression and WWII. He grew up a privileged child in the Hudson Valley. At Harvard, though only a C student, he edited the school paper and graduated in three years. He married Eleanor in 1905, became a lawyer in NYC, won a seat in the state senate, and was appointed Assistant Secretary of the Navy. He ran for vice president in 1920 but lost. He became NY governor in 1928, then in 1932 beat Herbert Hoover for the presidency. But the country was in peril: there were few jobs and little hope. He famously told America, "The only thing we have to fear is fear itself," and went on to help restore America through government-funded work. In 1941 Japan attacked Pearl Harbor as the Germans were overtaking Europe. Roosevelt led the U.S. into war. After four years, the U.S. was in position to win, but FDR died just before total victory. With Washington and Lincoln, he is considered one of our three greatest presidents.

BIO BITS
- He and Eleanor Roosevelt had six children.
- Struck by polio in 1921, he hid it from the public and used a wheelchair.
- At age 5, his father took him to visit President Grover Cleveland in the White House.

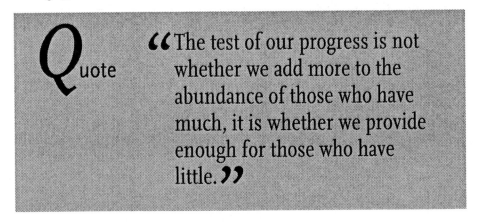

*Q*uote **"The test of our progress is not whether we add more to the abundance of those who have much, it is whether we provide enough for those who have little."**

ELEANOR ROOSEVELT

BORN: 10/11/1884
DIED: 11/7/1962
OCCUPATION: First Lady, Public Servant and Activist

Born in New York City, she was a tireless worker for the poor and the voiceless. Her father was Teddy Roosevelt's younger brother. Both her parents died by the time she was 10. She was sent to school in England and returned at age 18, mature and confident. In NYC, she was a volunteer teacher for immigrant children and fought to make working conditions safer in factories. She married her distant cousin, FDR, in 1905 and raised six children. As Franklin's career progressed, she actively advanced social causes. When FDR became president in 1933 at the start of the Great Depression, she spoke strongly for the young, poor, and for human rights. She was one of the first women to use the media for progressive causes and was often criticized for it. In 1945 she was appointed as a delegate to the United Nations by President Truman and served nine years. She helped to write the United Nation's Declaration of Human Rights. President Kennedy also called on her to advise for the Peace Corps. She was an outspoken and highly esteemed humanitarian until her death.

BIO BITS

- Franklin Delano Roosevelt was her fifth cousin.
- During WWI, she worked for the Red Cross.
- She wrote three books and had her own newspaper column, "My Day."

*Q*uote **"A woman is like a tea bag—you can't tell how strong she is until you put her in hot water."**

THEODORE ROOSEVELT

BORN: 10/27/1858
DIED: 1/6/1919
OCCUPATION: Public Servant and Reformer

Born on East 20th Street in Manhattan, he was a sickly, asthmatic child—which made him work harder his whole life to be fit. At age nine he created his own museum with animals he'd taxidermied, including the head of a dead seal from a fish market. His wealthy father took him traveling to Europe and Egypt. He went to Harvard, then to Columbia Law School. He moved to Montana for three years and lived on a ranch that he built but left when a terrible winter killed all his cattle. He came East, married, and was named NYC police commissioner. He was a big-time reformer. He worked for the Navy and led the Rough Riders in a war victory over Cuba. He was selected vice president in 1900, then when President McKinley died, he became president. He broke up powerful businesses, prosecuted corruption, regulated railroads, designed food and drug laws, and launched conservation programs for national parks. He served two terms, then went to Africa to hunt big game for a year. He ran again for president in 1912 but lost. He then made a famous South American expedition.

BIO BITS
- His father helped found the Metropolitan Museum of Art.
- He established the National Park Service along with its first National Park.
- The Teddy Bear is named after him, derived from a political cartoon.

*Q*uote **❝I am only an average man, but, by George, I work harder at it than the average man.❞**

DONALD J. TRUMP
BORN: 6/14/1946
DIED: —
OCCUPATION: Public Servant and Entrepreneur

Few thought he could win the presidency, yet he did. Born and raised in Queens, he went to school in NYC, then finished high school at the New York Military Academy. He went to college at Fordham for two years, then to the University of Pennsylvania. His family had a long history in real estate so he joined a firm run by his father. He became president of the company in the 1970s and the firm grew into a huge success. He was a tough negotiator and built hotel and real estate projects in NYC, as well as casinos and hotels in Atlantic City. He also built and managed golf courses around the world. For 14 seasons he produced and starred on TV in the wildly successful, *The Apprentice*, earning him fame and valuable media exposure. He ran for president with the slogan, "Make America Great Again." He was ridiculed during the campaign but spoke to the desires of concerned Americans in a savvy campaign. Though he lost the popular vote, he won the electoral college and 30 of the 50 states. His victory made him the oldest and wealthiest person ever to become president.

BIO BITS
- His grandfather immigrated to the U.S. at age 16 and made a fortune during the Gold Rush operating restaurants and boarding houses.
- He was scouted by professional baseball teams to play for them.
- From 1996–2015 he owned parts of the Miss Universe and Miss USA beauty pageants.

Q uote **" Sometimes by losing a battle you find a new way to win a war. "**

FRANCES PERKINS
BORN: 4/10/1880
DIED: 5/14/1965
OCCUPATION: Public Servant and Sociologist

A tireless protector of workers' welfare, she was the first woman appointed to a cabinet position. Born in Boston, she came to NYC to earn her master's degree at Columbia in 1910. After that she headed the city's Consumer League, fighting for better hours and working conditions. She personally witnessed the Triangle Shirtwaist fire, which changed her forever. She helped run NYC's Committee on Safety, then joined the Industrial Commission. FDR appointed her the first Commissioner of the state's Department of Labor in 1929. She reduced the work week for women to 48 hours, fought for a minimum wage, and put an end to child labor. FDR, as President in 1933, appointed her Secretary of the Department of Labor, a first for a woman. She ran it for 12 years, longer than any other. She helped write New Deal legislation, organized the Civilian Conservation Corps, and drafted the Social Security Act. President Truman appointed her to the U.S. Civil Service Commission, where she served from 1945–1952. She then taught at Cornell and other schools.

BIO BITS
- Her husband was frequently institutionalized for mental illness.
- She appeared on the cover of *Time* magazine in 1933.
- She established the first minimum wage and overtime laws for workers.

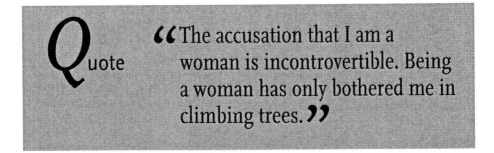

*Q*uote **"The accusation that I am a woman is incontrovertible. Being a woman has only bothered me in climbing trees."**

MARIO CUOMO

BORN: 6/15/1932
DIED: 12/31/2015
OCCUPATION: Public Servant

He might have been president but never ran. Born in Queens, both his parents were Italian immigrants who ran a family store. He went to P.S. 50 and college at St. John's, where he played baseball so well that he got a $2,000 signing bonus with the Pittsburgh Pirates. (He used the money to buy an engagement ring for his wife.) He stopped playing baseball when he was hit in the head by a pitch and spent six days in a hospital. He became a lawyer, then ran for mayor in 1977 but lost to Ed Koch. He was elected governor in 1982, the first of three terms. In 1984 he delivered the keynote address at the Democratic Convention and so electrified the crowd that many thought he would seek the presidency, but he decided not to run. As governor, his leadership helped stabilize New York during the crime-ridden decade of the 1980s, and he notably improved the education of children. He never lost his progressive fire and stood for liberal values to the last.

BIO BITS

- He spoke only Italian at home until starting public school.
- He was about to be offered a Supreme Court seat in 1993 by President Clinton but he withdrew himself from consideration.
- His son, Andrew, also became governor of New York.

*Q*uote **"** Every time I recall the early days, it's painful ... summoning up the terribly, terribly difficult life of my parents. And it's painful because I didn't realize at the time how hard it was for them. **"**

34

HENRY KISSINGER
BORN: 5/27/1923
DIED: —
OCCUPATION: Public Servant, Diplomat, Author

He was a German-born Jew who escaped the Nazis, then went on to become one of the most important diplomats in history. He fled the Nazis with his family in 1938 during a profoundly dangerous time. He arrived in NYC and lived in Washington Heights. He worked in a factory and went to high school at night. He went to City College, then was drafted into the army in 1943. He fought in the Battle of the Bulge and won a Bronze Star. He came back and went to Harvard, where he got his B.A., M.A. and his Ph.D. He was made faculty at Harvard and was a government consultant. He was an advisor to Governor Nelson Rockefeller during his runs for president. When Nixon won, he selected Kissinger for his National Security Advisor, then made him Secretary of State. He embraced a policy of détente, which relaxed tensions with the Soviet Union and formalized relations with Communist China. He was awarded the 1973 Nobel Peace Prize in part for the U.S.'s withdrawal from Vietnam. He continued as Secretary of State under President Ford.

BIO BITS
- His father was a teacher who lost his career under Nazi persecution.
- While in the U.S. army in Germany, he headed a team to track down and capture members of the Gestapo.
- He has written three memoirs and 14 books on foreign policy.

*Q*uote **"If you don't know where you are going, every road will get you nowhere."**

Preservationists

MARGOT GAYLE

BORN: 5/14/1908
DIED: 9/28/2008
OCCUPATION: Preservationist

She is known as the woman who saved Soho. Gayle was born in Kansas City while her father worked in the nascent auto industry. She moved with her husband to New York after WWII and was employed by CBS radio, then she wrote a column about architecture for *The Daily News*. She first saved a cast-iron clock on the Jefferson Market Courthouse, then became a major voice for protecting New York landmarks and assisting in passing preservation laws. Gayle founded *The Friends of Cast Iron Architecture* in 1970. One of her great accomplishments was helping stop a planned expressway that was designed to run right through Soho on a path along Broome Street. Because of her protests, the freeway was never built and Soho remains historically preserved. She went on national campaigns to protect cast-iron buildings around the country and helped save other clocks in Manhattan and Brooklyn. She ran for City Council and dressed up as a suffragist with her two daughters. She lost that race but never lost her spunk to help save the architectural history of New York.

BIO BITS

- She lived to be 100.
- She received her master's degree in Bacteriology from Emory University.
- She assisted in saving photographic treasures from the Alice Austen House in Staten Island.

*Q*uote **" That's the price of getting something saved. There's got to be money in it for someone. "**

JANE JACOBS
BORN: 5/4/1916
DIED: 4/25/2006
OCCUPATION: Preservationist and Author

How could a woman without a college degree do so much to save neighborhoods? Born in Scranton, PA, a doctor's daughter, she moved to NYC in the middle of the Great Depression. She fell in love with Greenwich Village because it didn't fit into the grid of city streets. She was a freelance writer, which helped her learn about the city. She worked for the government during WWII. In the 1950s she took a job with *Architectural Forum*, leading her to question urban planning: she saw how it destroyed community life. In 1961 Jacobs published *The Death and Life of Great American Cities*, called by many the most influential book ever written on city planning. Developers were outraged. She was called a "militant dame" and "housewife." When the Lower Manhattan Expressway was planned to be built in the 1960s, going right through Washington Square Park, she blocked the project as much as anyone through her organizing. She witnessed life from her home above a candy store at 555 Hudson Street and that, as much as anything, created her urban planning philosophy.

BIO BITS

- Jane Jacobs Day is celebrated every year on June 28th.
- She was arrested in 1968 for trying to stop the LOMAX expressway.
- She moved to Toronto to prevent her two sons from being drafted into the Vietnam War.

Quote **"Cities have the capability of providing something for everybody, only because, and only when, they are created by everybody."**

MATHEW BRADY

BORN: 5/18/1822
DIED: 1/15/1896
OCCUPATION: Preservationist Photographer

He should have been a very wealthy man but died deep in debt. Brady's parents were Irish immigrants when he was born in upstate New York. He painted portraits and, at age 16, moved to Saratoga. Daguerreotypes (early photography) came to NYC in 1839 and Brady became a student of them. In 1844 he opened a studio and took portraits of Daniel Webster, Edgar Allan Poe, Andrew Jackson and John Quincy Adams. He moved to Staten Island in 1851, won photography awards, then made money taking soldiers' photos before they left for the Civil War. Brady received permission to carry his photographic studio to war sites to document the battlefield. His staff captured thousands of Civil War scenes, which assists our current understanding of the war. Photos of dead people were seen for the first time and the public was horrified. He spent $100,000 on plates to photograph Civil War scenes, but the government did not buy them from him afterward, so Brady went bankrupt. He died penniless in a charity ward at Presbyterian Hospital after a streetcar accident.

BIO BITS

- He is known as the father of photojournalism.
- He photographed 18 different American presidents.
- Mathew Brady and his studio produced over 7,000 pictures.

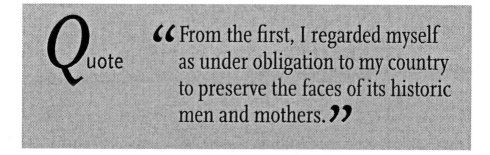

*Q*uote **"From the first, I regarded myself as under obligation to my country to preserve the faces of its historic men and mothers."**

JACQUELINE KENNEDY ONASSIS
BORN: 7/28/1929
DIED: 5/19/1994
OCCUPATION: Preservationist and First Lady

She transformed the role of First Lady into an important part of every presidency. Born on Long Island, her father was a rich Wall Street banker. At age 11 she won an equestrian championship. She went to boarding school in Connecticut, then to Vassar College. While working in D.C. in 1952, she met John F. Kennedy, a young congressman. He asked for a date and they married a year later. JFK won the presidency in 1960 and, from her love of history, it became her mission to restore the White House to a type of museum to inspire patriotism. As First Lady, Onassis brought attention to the arts and created international goodwill due to her skill with foreign leaders. She was a national asset. When JFK was assassinated, America took solace in her strength during one of America's most trying times. She returned to NYC permanently in 1975 and became a supporter of the arts, a book publisher, and an architectural preservationist. She led a campaign to stop the demolition of Grand Central Terminal and restore it to its current beautiful condition.

BIO BITS

- Her birth name was Jacqueline Lee Bouvier and she was baptized as Catholic in Manhattan.
- She was fluent in French, Spanish and Italian.
- She won an Emmy Award in 1962 for her televised tour of the White House.

*Q*uote **"A great goal in life is the only fortune worth finding."**

RUTH WITTENBERG

BORN: 1899
DIED: 10/1/1990
OCCUPATION: Preservationist

Though she was jailed twice, she would not be held back. She was born in Brooklyn and part of an activist family. In fact, she was set on the knee of Socialist Eugene V. Debs as a child. She marched as a suffragette before 1919 and was twice jailed. She attended Hunter College and Barnard but had to quit to support her family with a job at Bell Telephone. She married in 1919. In 1951 she was appointed to the Community Council for Greenwich Village and fought for historic preservation. Wittenberg had a women's detention center removed and replaced with a garden—sustaining the area's character. Park Commissioner Robert Moses wanted Fifth Avenue to run through Washington Square Park but, with her assistance in a grassroots effort, all traffic was cleared from the park in 1963. She continued to fight development and retain community character in long battles with city officials—leading to the Jefferson Market Courthouse and Greenwich Village becoming designated Historic Districts. She served on Community Board 2 for almost 40 years and did battle for her neighborhood to preserve its character and history.

BIO BITS

- At age 66 she traveled to Alabama and marched with Dr. Martin Luther King.
- Ruth Wittenberg Triangle on Greenwich Avenue is named for her.
- Community Board meetings were held in her hospital room when she was sick.

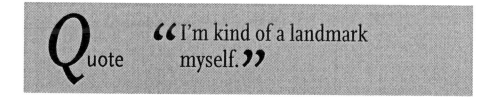

*Q*uote **"I'm kind of a landmark myself."**

Entrepreneurs

DOROTHY SCHIFF

BORN: 3/11/1903
DIED: 8/30/1989
OCCUPATION: Newspaper Publisher

She was scrappy and smart enough to run a major paper for nearly 40 years. Born into a wealthy German-Jewish banking family, she said that she had no joy growing up. Raised on the Upper East Side, she attended the Brearely School, then Bryn Mawr College, where she claimed that she flunked every class. Her first marriage failed. Her second husband talked her into taking over *The New York Post*, a struggling afternoon daily. She did and lost nearly $2 million the first two years. Her editor said that the chance that the paper would survive were one in a thousand. But she cut costs and, from 1950 on, *The Post* made money almost every year. It was New York's "liberal" paper. Her competition collapsed and *The Post* became the sole afternoon daily. She didn't give employees kind words or bonuses for she said, "They weren't given to me as a child, and any words I did receive were not ones of praise." She sold *The Post* in 1976 to Rupert Murdoch for $31 million. She called running a newspaper "a terrible headache" but she outlasted many men.

BIO BITS

- She had four husbands, all of whom she divorced.
- After selling her paper, she said she preferred doing needlepoint.
- She was a good friend, when young, of President Franklin Roosevelt.

*Q*uote **"In those days, I thought it was important to be married, and since the substantial older ones had enough sense not to marry me, there wasn't much choice."**

41

PETER COOPER
BORN: 2/12/1791
DIED: 4/4/1883
OCCUPATION: Industrialist and Philanthropist

He was a tinkerer as a boy and his curiosity led him to become one of the world's richest men. His father made hats. As a young man, Cooper had many inventions that didn't make much money. Then in 1821 he purchased a factory in Kips Bay, Manhattan that produced glues and paints from slaughterhouse animals. It did well. He then bought land in Maryland to extract iron ore to make railroad rails. That earned his first fortune. He opened an iron rolling mill in NYC in 1836 and expanded to Trenton, employing 2,000 people. Cooper invested in real estate and insurance and became among the richest men in NYC. But he was frugal. He wore simple clothes and had only two servants. In 1855 he formed the American Telegraph Company and in 1858 it laid transatlantic cable. He was ardently against slavery, aided Indians, and in 1876 ran for president at age 85. He had a lifelong interest in education and in 1859 opened Cooper Union, a private college primarily for students of art and engineering. It had no tuition until 2014 and even now is almost free.

BIO BITS
- He had six children but only two survived past the age of four.
- He founded Children's Village, one of the oldest non-profit charities in NYC.
- He died at age 92 and is buried in Green-Wood Cemetery in Brooklyn.

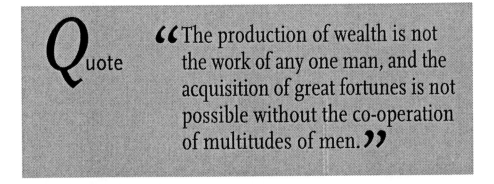

Quote **"The production of wealth is not the work of any one man, and the acquisition of great fortunes is not possible without the co-operation of multitudes of men."**

MADAM C.J. WALKER
BORN: 12/23/1867
DIED: 5/25/1919
OCCUPATION: Entrepreneur and Activist

Who would have thought one of the first women to be a self-made millionaire would have been African American? Both her parents died by the time she was seven. She moved in with family and picked cotton. She married and had a daughter at age 18. Her husband died. She moved to St. Louis to live with her brothers. There, she met and married Charles J. Walker. Her hair fell out due to a scalp ailment so she experimented with products to help her heal. They worked! She developed and sold them to other African Americans. By 1910 her business was incredibly successful. In 1913 she purchased a property in Harlem as a base for operations. In Harlem she established philanthropies, gave scholarships to the poor, provided housing for the elderly, and supported the NAACP and the National Conference on Lynching. During WWI, her assistance greatly aided the Circle for Negro War Relief; she also tried to establish a camp to train black officers in the U.S. Army. Her rise from cotton picker to major social promoter was as far as anyone has traveled.

BIO BITS
- Both of her parents were freed slaves.
- In 1998 a stamp was issued in her honor by the U.S. Postal Service.
- She is buried in Woodlawn Cemetery in the Bronx.

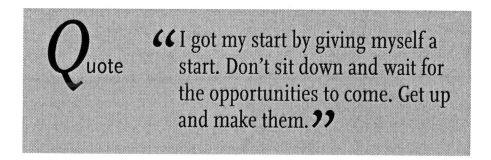

Quote **" I got my start by giving myself a start. Don't sit down and wait for the opportunities to come. Get up and make them. "**

43

EMILY AND WASHINGTON ROEBLING
BORN: 9/23/1843 (E) and 5/26/1837 (W)
DIED: 2/28/1903 (E) and 7/21/1926 (W)
OCCUPATION: Engineers and Bridge Builders

Emily became the woman who saved the Brooklyn Bridge. Born in Putnam County, one of a dozen children, she met her husband, Washington, in 1864 in D.C. while he served in the Civil War. They married a year later. His father, John Roebling, was hired to build the Brooklyn Bridge in 1869 but an on-sight accident led to his death that year. His son took over but he became gravely ill from the bends in 1870 when he was trapped in a caisson during a fire. Washington could barely speak and did not return to the site. Emily led all aspects of construction while he speechlessly gave instruction. She learned engineering and saw to daily planning. He advised as he could from home. It took 13 years, with his communicating details and her on-sight management, but the project finished. The Brooklyn Bridge opened in 1883 and 150,000 people crossed it. Many thought Emily designed it because of her role in the astounding engineering feat. President Arthur walked the bridge, came to the Roebling house, and shook Washington's hand, though he was still ill.

BIO BITS
- He saw military action in five Civil War battles, including Gettysburg.
- She traveled to Russia in 1896 for the coronation of Tsar Nicholas II.
- She continued her education and received a law degree from New York University.

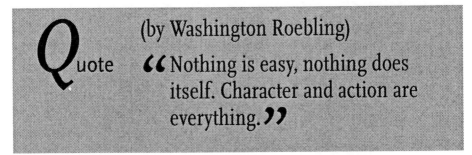

Quote (by Washington Roebling) **"**Nothing is easy, nothing does itself. Character and action are everything.**"**

44

GEORGE STEINBRENNER

BORN: 7/4/1930
DIED: 7/13/2010
OCCUPATION: Baseball Owner

His father never accepted failure and he had the same attitude as owner of the New York Yankees for 37 years. His dad told him: work harder than anyone who works for you. He did. From age nine, Steinbrenner began his own business in Ohio selling chickens door-to-door. He made good money. He was a track star at Williams College, edited the school paper, and played in the band. In 1952 he went into the Air Force. After that, with a love of sports, he bought a minor league basketball team: it ended up losing $25 million! But Steinbrenner didn't give up. In 1973, the Yankees were a poor team and he was able to purchase it in a partnership for $10 million. He drove his employees hard but his uncompromising attitude of "always win" began a string of seasons that made the Yankees the most feared team in baseball. He had a military-style grooming code: players must be clean-shaven and hair could not grow over the collar. He had legal difficulties and personal faults but he gave his all to make the Yankees the most successful franchise ever in any sport.

BIO BITS
- The Yankees employed 19 managers in his time because he fired so many.
- The Yankees won seven World Series and 11 pennants while he was the owner.
- He invested in six Broadway shows and they were mostly flops.

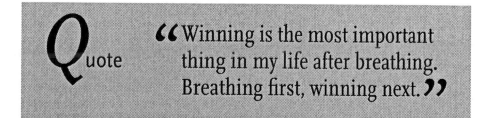

*Q*uote **"Winning is the most important thing in my life after breathing. Breathing first, winning next."**

JOSEPH "JOE" PAPP
BORN: 6/22/1921
DIED: 10/31/1991
OCCUPATION: Theatre Producer

Born in Williamsburg to Shmuel and Yetta Papirof-sky, he spoke only Yiddish until he learned English playing in city streets. His family was so poor that he had to shine shoes and pluck chickens for money. He was often beaten up and regularly had to move because his parents could not pay the rent. He joined the Navy in WWII and produced shows on ships. He came back to NYC in 1948. In 1954 he produced free Shakespeare in a church on the Lower East Side. In 1956 the Parks Department let him use the East River Park in a 2,000 seat amphitheatre. (Actors were not paid.) The next year a mobile theatre landed in Central Park where the Delacourte Theatre (opened in 1962) now sits. He took over the Astor Library in 1966 on Lafayette Street for The Public Theatre and created six performance spaces inside. He had hit shows (*A Chorus Line, Hair*) that went to Broadway and made the theatre a lot of money. He often battled mayors and civil servants to make his art. No one has produced so much free theatre for NYC and his legacy will live forever.

BIO BITS
- His parents were Jewish immigrants from Russia and his dad made trunks.
- He led the "Save the Theatres" movement that stopped landmark Broadway houses from destruction.
- He is buried in the Baron Hirsch Cemetery on Staten Island.

Quote **"When the moon is out and the wind begins to whisper, it's theater at its best."**

FREDERICK LAW OLMSTEAD
BORN: 8/26/1822
DIED: 8/28/1903
OCCUPATION: Landscape Architect

The beauty of Central Park depended upon him. Born in Connecticut, his mother died before he was four. His father loved nature and cultivated that in his son. Olmstead became a seaman and merchant, then settled on Staten Island in 1848 on a 125 acre farm. (His home at 4515 Hylan Boulevard still stands.) He entered journalism and wrote extensively about parks, then traveled to the South to write about slavery before the Civil War. He entered a competition to design Central Park with Calvert Vaux and the duo won in 1858. Their Central Park plan was put into place and building quickly began. Olmstead wanted common green space so that all citizens had access without the invasion of private interests. He wanted a "People's Park." After completion, the duo went on to design Brooklyn's Prospect Park in 1865. Olmstead worked for the government during the Civil War and headed a medical effort for the sick and wounded. He also designed city parks for Chicago, Buffalo and Milwaukee. He was among the earliest leaders of the conservation movement.

BIO BITS
- He almost went to Yale but got sumac poisoning and had to withdraw due to bad eyesight.
- He led the U.S. Sanitary Commission (the Red Cross) during the Civil War.
- He designed Ocean Parkway, as well as many campuses in the U.S. including Stanford University.

Quote **"**Gradually and silently the charm comes over us; we know not exactly where or how.**"**

FRED LEBOW
BORN: 6/3/1932
DIED: 10/9/1994
OCCUPATION: Sports Organizer

How could a small man born in Transylvania become the founder of an event that causes such good feelings in New York? He was born Fischl Lebowitz and survived the WWII Nazi occupation. He made his way to New York in the early '60s and attended the Fashion Institute of Technology. He first loved tennis, then switched to running because he said it would be immoral not to let everyone know how great it is. He founded the New York City Marathon in 1970 and spent much of his own money to start it: $300 of a total $1,000 budget. The race was only in Central Park and was a four-lap tour. 127 runners started and 55 finished. Lebow ran a 4:12:55. Six years later, the marathon included all five boroughs. Today, the NYC Marathon is always held on the first Sunday in November and is a spectacular event, drawing 50,000 runners from around the world. The best runners compete for a $100,000 first prize. That prize is amazing when you realize what was spent on the first marathon. Lebow is one of the most beloved sports figures in NYC's history.

BIO BITS
- In his first marathon, he finished 45th out of 55 runners.
- He completed 69 marathons in 30 countries during his lifetime.
- Prizes for the first marathon included recycled bowling trophies.

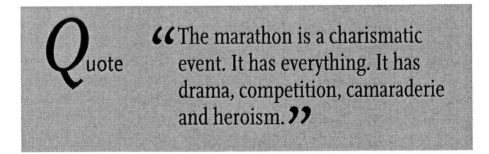

*Q*uote **"The marathon is a charismatic event. It has everything. It has drama, competition, camaraderie and heroism."**

CORNELIUS VANDERBILT

BORN: 5/27/1794
DIED: 1/4/1877
OCCUPATION: Entrepreneur

He was the son of a poor waterman who grew up on Staten Island and later became among the richest men ever. He quit school at age 11 to work for his father's ferry business. At 16 he started his own ferry company between Staten Island and Manhattan. He married his cousin at 19 and moved to Manhattan. While running his own ferry, he also managed a ferry between New Jersey and NYC—and there learned how to grow a business. He expanded his water services to Long Island Sound and the Hudson River during a time when industry was rapidly expanding. He undercut the prices of others and provided better service. He took control of railroads in the 1840s, then steamship lines running from Panama to California. He invested massively in real estate in NYC. He purchased major shipyards in the 1850s. During the Civil War, he donated his largest steamship to the Union cause. He continued to grow, expand and consolidate his railroad lines on the East Coast until they dominated the U.S. At the time of his death, he was worth over $150 billion in today's dollars.

BIO BITS

- He gave $1 million to start Vanderbilt University: the largest charitable gift ever at the time.
- His last residence was at 10 Washington Place near Washington Square Park.
- All of his family's wealth was virtually gone within four generations.

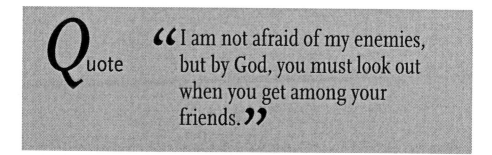

Quote **"**I am not afraid of my enemies, but by God, you must look out when you get among your friends.**"**

Scientists and Explorers

49

GIOVANNI DA VERRAZZANO
BORN: C. 1485
DIED: C. 1528
OCCUPATION: Explorer

Though born in Italy, he worked for France and became the first southern European to explore the NYC area. He sought adventure from an early age and sailed to Egypt and Syria. Verrazzano was then sent by French king Francis I to sail to the New World. They hoped to find a route to China and make money trading spices. Instead, he ran into our East Coast and discovered inlets around New York. He met the Lenape Indians at the entrance to the Hudson River. He sailed along Long Island and met the Wampananoag and Narragansett Indians. Verrazzano left diaries about his voyages with precise descriptions. He named the new land "Francesca" after the king who sponsored him. He thought the inlets might lead to China so he returned to France to prepare a second voyage. However, on this second trip he ended up in Brazil. He made a third sailing voyage to the New World with his brother and that did not go well. He was captured by cannibals off the coast of Florida. His brother, still on the ship at sea, watched from afar as they roasted Verrazzano and ate him.

BIO BITS
- The Verrazano-Narrows Bridge connects Brooklyn to Staten Island.
- He explored the Hudson River nearly 100 years before Henry Hudson.
- He discovered the Cape Cod Bay and made an accurate map of it.

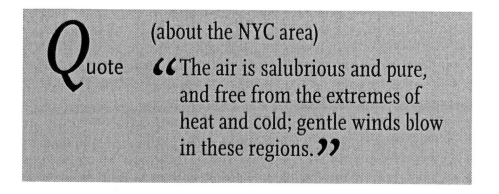

Q uote (about the NYC area)

" The air is salubrious and pure, and free from the extremes of heat and cold; gentle winds blow in these regions. "

J. ROBERT OPPENHEIMER

BORN: 4/22/1904
DIED: 2/18/1967
OCCUPATION: Physicist

He is the father of the atomic bomb that killed many thousands yet may have saved millions of lives. He was born in New York. His father was a German immigrant who spoke no English when he arrived, yet he advanced quickly in business to become wealthy. The family moved to 155 Riverside Drive in 1912. Oppenheimer went to the Ethical Culture Society School, then Harvard, where he explored physics and graduated in three years. He was brilliant and went to Cambridge, Caltech, then taught at Berkeley. When WWII broke out Oppenheimer was named to head the Manhattan Project, which was a daunting effort to develop an atomic bomb before Germany did. It required scientists in many fields working together and took four years of round-the-clock labor to develop. Finally, a successful atomic bomb test took place in 1945 in the desert of New Mexico. Soon the bomb was dropped on Hiroshima and Nagasaki and Japan surrendered. WWII was over. Had the U.S. not gotten Japan to surrender, it is speculated that millions of lives would have been lost as the war continued.

BIO BITS
- His father made so much money that he bought three van Gogh paintings.
- He had a ranch out West and loved horseback riding.
- He learned the Sanskrit language in 1933 and read the Bhagavad Gita in it.

*Q*uote **"The scientist is free, and must be free to ask any question, to doubt any assertion, to seek for any evidence, to correct any errors."**

PETER MINUIT

BORN: c. 1580–1585
DIED: 1638
OCCUPATION: Explorer and Administrator

Born in the Netherlands, his family had to flee Spanish Catholic colonists to Germany because they were Protestant. He married in 1613. His wife was rich and helped him get established in business. He joined the Dutch West India Company around 1625 and sailed to the New World to become a trader. As director of New Netherland, in 1626 he purchased the island of Manhattan from the Lenape Indians for trinkets valued at 60 guilders. Today that equals about $1,000! Minuit went on to buy Staten Island from other Indians in exchange for iron tools, kettles, trinkets and cloth. As the chief administrator of New Netherland, Minuit made trading decisions and was also the land's highest judge. Commerce grew quickly under his leadership and eventually there were 300 people in the new colony. He returned home to Europe in 1632 and was fired from running the colony likely because he helped fur traders not associated with the Dutch West India Company. He returned to the New World in 1636 to establish a Swedish colony on the lower Delaware River.

BIO BITS

- His surname, "Minuit," means *Midnight*.
- As a young man he was a diamond cutter in the Dutch city of Utrecht.
- He died on a voyage during a hurricane in the Caribbean.

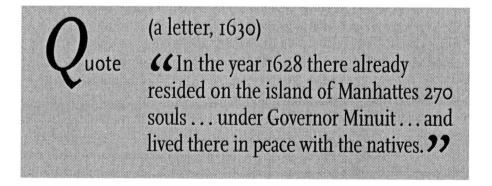

Quote   (a letter, 1630)

❝ In the year 1628 there already resided on the island of Manhattes 270 souls ... under Governor Minuit ... and lived there in peace with the natives. ❞

52

ROBERT FULTON

BORN: 11/14/1765
DIED: 2/24/1815
OCCUPATION: Inventor and Engineer

Though his parents were Irish immigrants, he went on to produce the first workable steamboat and submarine. His dad went bankrupt and died when Fulton was nine. He was sent to a Quaker school in Pennsylvania. His elders saw that he was good at painting so sent him to London to study art but he was not well received. He got interested in inventions, especially canals and propelled boats, so he designed torpedoes and submarines. He went to France to build the Nautilus sub and in 1797 it submersed for 17 minutes. In 1807 he built the famous steamboat Clermont, which carried passengers 150 miles between NYC and Albany in 32 hours. Before that it took four days for sailboats to make the voyage. Fulton's development made steamboats viable for transportation. In 1812 he was on the commission that recommended building the Erie Canal. He continued to support the U.S. in engineering boats for naval defense. Fulton died of pneumonia and tuberculosis after jumping in freezing water to rescue his friend who fell through ice in the Hudson River.

BIO BITS

- When young, his job was painting portraits on lockets in Philadelphia.
- He is buried in Trinity Church Cemetery near Wall Street.
- Fulton Street in Manhattan is named after him.

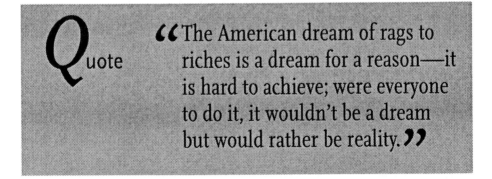

*Q*uote **"**The American dream of rags to riches is a dream for a reason—it is hard to achieve; were everyone to do it, it wouldn't be a dream but would rather be reality.**"**

DAVID HO
BORN: 11/3/1952
DIED: —
OCCUPATION: Scientist and Academic

From the mid-1980s through the 1990s, HIV/AIDS was one of the most frightening diseases in the world. It was not well understood. Dr. Ho's groundbreaking research changed the way the disease was treated worldwide. Born in Taiwan, China, he moved to California when he was 12. He was raised in California, then later went to Harvard and became a doctor. He researched HIV/AIDS and discovered that the virus massively reproduces in the body immediately after infection. It was previously assumed that the virus waited to reproduce so treatments were withheld until the symptoms became visible. With Dr. Ho's discovery, a "cocktail" of drugs was given to those infected and it significantly improved survival rates. He spent over 30 years as a world leader on AIDS research and has published over 400 papers and received 12 honorary doctorate degrees. Today he is a scientific director at the Rockefeller University in New York. In 2006 he was inducted into the California Hall of Fame.

BIO BITS
- He was named *Time* magazine's "Man of the Year" in 1996 for his discoveries and the many lives that he saved.
- His father worked in China as a translator for U.S. troops during WWII and immigrated to America in the mid-1950s.
- He lives in New York with his wife, an artist, and their three children.

> Q
> uote
> **" My training has been entirely American, while culturally I am a large part Chinese. "**

PETER STUYVESANT

BORN: C. 1592
DIED: August, 1672
OCCUPATION: Explorer and Public Servant

A cannonball blew off his leg when he was young but that didn't stop "Peg Leg Pete" from becoming an important early leader. He was born in the Netherlands. In 1645 he was appointed Director-General of New Netherland—what we now call New York. He used brutality and violence to rule the land and stop the insurrections led by his own Dutch people, many Swedes, and Indians. Finally, the English conquered his colony and Stuyvesant handed his city over to them. That occurred because his own Dutch citizens, who loathed him, refused to help defend him against British warships! They wanted Stuyvesant to lose. So he had to surrender the city to the British, who then changed the city's name New York. Stuyvesant was strict because he had to establish order in a new civilization. Colonizers came from all over the globe and the population grew from 2,000 to 8,000 while he managed the colony. Because he established a strict order, trade benefited and that helped grow New York into the city that it is today: an economic and cultural powerhouse.

BIO BITS

- His last direct descendent, August Stuyvesant, died at 83 in 1953 in NYC.
- He retired to a farm on land that is now the Bowery and lived there until he died.
- One of the most famous high schools in Manhattan is named for him.

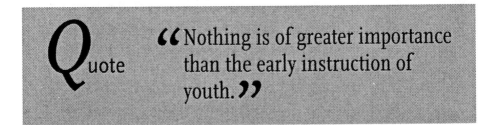

Quote **"Nothing is of greater importance than the early instruction of youth."**

JONAS SALK
BORN: 10/28/1914
DIED: 6/23/1995
OCCUPATION: Medical Researcher

He saved countless children from being crippled at a time of panic in America. His parents were Jewish immigrants from Russia. His father worked in the garment district. The poor family lived in East Harlem, Queens and the Bronx. He graduated from Townsend Harris High School at age 15, then went to NYU to study medicine. But he really wanted to be a scientist. Jews faced discrimination in this period so it took time for him to secure another research position. Finally, Salk was hired at Michigan to work on the flu virus. He then went to Pittsburgh to open his own laboratory. When offered the chance to work on the polio virus, Salk jumped on it. Polio was an epidemic afflicting children like a plague and scientists couldn't figure it out. Salk worked 16 hours a day, seven days a week, for years. He created a vaccine and, in 1952, injected his family and over 50 children with it. In 1955, after years of testing, the vaccine was determined safe. He was celebrated as a national hero.

BIO BITS

- In 1952, more than 58,000 cases of polio were reported, paralyzing 21,000.
- President Reagan declared May 6, 1985 as "Jonas Salk Day" to honor him.
- He opened the Salk Institute in 1963 to assist budding scientists with their careers.

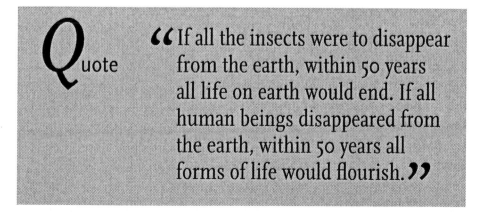

Q*uote* **" If all the insects were to disappear from the earth, within 50 years all life on earth would end. If all human beings disappeared from the earth, within 50 years all forms of life would flourish. "**

SUSAN McKINNEY-STEWARD
BORN: March, 1847
DIED: 3/17/1918
OCCUPATION: Doctor and Advocate

Born in Crown Heights, she was the seventh of 10 children and became New York's first female African American to earn a medical degree. She was of mixed race: African, Shinnecock Indian and European. She attended the New York Medical College for Women at age 20 and had her medical degree in three years (class valedictorian). She stayed in Brooklyn and ran a medical practice for 25 years serving African Americans. She helped found the Brooklyn Women's Homeopathic Hospital at that time. Part of her practice was at the Brooklyn Home for Aged Colored People, where she served on the board of directors. In 1892 she began practicing at the New York Medical College and the Hospital for Women in Manhattan. She was a specialist as a pediatrician and concentrated on childhood diseases and prenatal care. She fought for human rights, women's suffrage, as well as temperance. An excellent public speaker, she addressed the first Universal Race Congress in London in 1911. She finished her life as a teacher for 22 years at Wilberforce University in Ohio.

BIO BITS
- Her sister, Sarah Garnet, was NYC's first African-American school principal.
- Two of her Brooklyn-born brothers died in the Civil War.
- She is interred in Green-Wood Cemetery in Brooklyn.

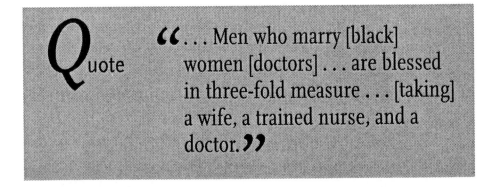

*Q*uote **"** . . . Men who marry [black] women [doctors] . . . are blessed in three-fold measure . . . [taking] a wife, a trained nurse, and a doctor. **"**

57

HENRY HUDSON

BORN: 1565–70
DIED: 1611
OCCUPATION: Explorer

He was trying to find a passage to China when he sailed the river that was given his name. Not much is known about Hudson's early life. He is from England. He probably started as a cabin boy and earned his way up to captain. In 1609 he was hired to sail for the Dutch East India Company to find a route to Asia. He reached Manhattan on his ship, the Half Moon, and sailed up the Hudson to what is now Albany. He traded with Indians along the way and his logs and commercial notes were used by the Dutch to establish land claims for a colony. His maps and directions led the Dutch to found a profitable trading post in Albany in 1614. Because of him, New Amsterdam (Manhattan) became the capital of New Netherland. From 1610–11 Hudson made another voyage, this time for the English. On this trip his ship reached what is now named the Hudson Bay in Canada. However, his crew mutinied and put Hudson, his son, and seven sick crew members into a small boat and cast them adrift in a bay in Canada. No signs of their fate have ever been discovered.

BIO BITS

- It is reported he married a woman named Katherine and they had three sons.
- He first explored for the English, then the Dutch, then for the English.
- His mutineers were put on trial for abandoning Hudson but were acquitted.

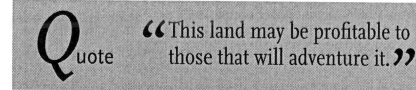

Quote **"**This land may be profitable to those that will adventure it.**"**

CARL SAGAN

BORN: 11/9/1934
DIED: 12/20/1996
OCCUPATION: Astronomer and Educator

His father was an immigrant garment worker from Ukraine who also worked as a movie usher. Sagan was born in Brooklyn and grew up in Bensonhurst. He was raised as a Reform Jew. His parents took him to the 1939 World's Fair and it generated his lifelong love of space. He was thrilled visiting the Hayden Planetarium and Museum of Natural History. His parents bought him chemistry sets to foster his interest in science. He went to Boody Junior High, then the family moved to New Jersey. He attended the University of Chicago at 16, then continued to get his Ph.D. He did post-grad work at Berkeley, then was hired by Harvard, then joined the faculty at Cornell. He advised NASA. His greatest impact came from co-writing and narrating a 13-part PBS series in 1980 titled, *Cosmos: A Personal Voyage.* It was the most watched public TV series in history, seen by over 500 million people in 60 countries. He appeared on many TV programs, advised astronauts, and had such charm and excitement for space exploration that it affected the nation and world.

BIO BITS

- He had his bar mitzvah in Brooklyn's Bensonhurst section when he turned 13.
- He was married three times and had five children.
- Isaac Asimov said that Sagan was one of only two people he met whose intellect surpassed his.

*Q*uote **❝**Every one of us is, in the cosmic perspective, precious. If a human disagrees with you, let him live. In a hundred billion galaxies, you will not find another.**❞**

MARGARET MEAD

BORN: 12/16/1901
DIED: 11/15/1978
OCCUPATION: Cultural Anthropologist

She is America's best known anthropologist. Born in Philadelphia to a family of intellectuals, she went to Barnard College in NYC for her bachelor's degree in 1923, then to Columbia for her master's in 1924. (She got her Ph.D. from Columbia in 1929.) In 1925 she spent a year in Samoa doing field studies, living among the people and learning the language. The product was her best-selling book, *Coming of Age in Samoa* in 1928. Her writing style made the book easy to read for regular people as well as scientists. It stated that the personalities of men and women are more determined by cultural conditioning than heredity. Mead lived in New Guinea next and published, *Growing Up in New Guinea* in 1930, also highly-regarded. She was named assistant curator at the American Museum of Natural History and held the position throughout her life. She traveled and published widely: 12 solo books and co-authored eight. She was given the Presidential Medal of Freedom posthumously in 1979 for her contribution to anthropology and human understanding.

BIO BITS

- She was married three times, once to a theology student and twice to anthropologists.
- She had one daughter who also became an anthropologist.
- P.S. 209 in Sheepshead Bay, Brooklyn, is named for her.

*Q*uote **❝ Never doubt that a small group of thoughtful, committed citizens can change the world; indeed, it's the only thing that ever has. ❞**

RICHARD FEYNMAN

BORN: 5/11/1918
DIED: 2/15/1988
OCCUPATION: Physicist and Writer

His father was a Belarus immigrant and he grew up to be one of the world's best-known scientists. Feynman was born in Queens in a non-religious Jewish family. He didn't speak a word until he was three. He loved repairing radios and built his own experimental lab as a boy. At 10 his family moved to Far Rockaway. At age 15 he taught himself advanced algebra, trigonometry, analytic geometry and calculus. He won the NYU math championship while in high school. Feynman went to MIT for his bachelor's, then to Princeton for his Ph.D. after achieving a perfect score on the graduate physics test. He took a position with the Manhattan Project during WWII, though he was barely 25. After the war he did research at Cornell and Caltech. He was co-awarded the Nobel Prize for Physics in 1965 for his work on quantum electrodynamics: tying together wave and particle phenomena in light, radio, electricity and magnetism. His 1985 book, *Surely You're Joking, Mr. Feynman!* became a best-seller. A group of physicists voted him among the 10 best physicists of all time.

BIO BITS

- He retained a thick Brooklyn accent throughout his life.
- Columbia turned him down for college because their quota for Jewish applicants was reached.
- He is renowned for his role on the panel investigating the Challenger spacecraft disaster and brought great understanding to the reasons it crashed.

Quote **"**The first principle is that you must not fool yourself and you are the easiest person to fool.**"**

NIKOLA TESLA
BORN: 7/10/1856
DIED: 1/7/1943
OCCUPATION: Inventor and Futurist

Mad scientist or pure genius? His father was an Orthodox priest in the Austrian Empire. During his school years, he stayed awake from 3 a.m. to 11 p.m. He became an electrician in Budapest, then got a job installing lighting in Paris in 1882. Edison's company brought him to NYC in 1884. He quit the company over a pay dispute. He tried to patent a lighting system, then worked for $2 a day as a ditch digger. In 1887 financial backers formed the Tesla Electric Company. He worked on motors and AC power systems. Westinghouse Company backed him and Tesla became wealthy. He set up labs on Grand Street, South Fifth Avenue and Houston Street. He built the Tesla Coil, helped generate power from Niagara Falls, did X-ray imaging and advanced wireless transmission. His memory was photographic. He rarely slept, was 6'2" and weighed 142 lbs., walked 8–10 miles per day, ate at exactly 8:10 every night, and lived in hotels. He was an oddball but brilliant. He died in the New Yorker Hotel at age 86. He never married and won a profound number of awards.

BIO BITS
- His mother was a genius and memorized epic Serbian poems by heart.
- He once spent $2,000 healing a beloved pigeon with a broken wing and leg.
- He was given a state funeral in the Catherdral of Saint John the Divine.

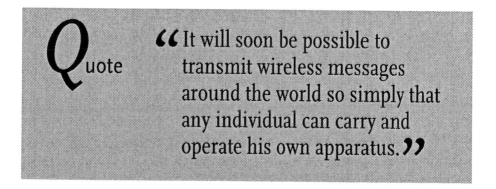

Q uote **"It will soon be possible to transmit wireless messages around the world so simply that any individual can carry and operate his own apparatus."**

JANET YELLEN
BORN: 8/13/1946
DIED: —
OCCUPATION: Economist, Educator, Public Servant

She is the most powerful female economist in U.S. history and heads the Federal Reserve System. She grew up in the Bay Ridge section of Brooklyn, the daughter of a Jewish doctor who worked from home. Her mother was a former school teacher. She graduated from Fort Hamilton High School and was editor of the school paper, class valedictorian, and took extra math classes at Columbia on Saturdays. She graduated from Brown in 1967, then received her Ph.D. from Yale in 1971. She went on to teach at Harvard and Berkeley. She was appointed to the Federal Reserve Board of Governors in 1994, then to the Federal Reserve Bank in 2004. In 2013 President Obama selected her as the first woman to lead the Federal Reserve, which helps determine how much money and lending is in the economy. It tries to be sure the nation has enough money to create jobs, but not so much that prices go sky high. It is the bank for the nation's banks, as well as for the federal government. As the head of the Federal Reserve, all American lives are affected by its monetary and lending decisions. She leads its group of economists.

BIO BITS

- She started collecting rocks at age eight and has over 200 different specimens.
- After high school, she was one of 29 students to receive a Regents scholarship.
- Her husband is also an economist and won a Nobel Prize in 2001.

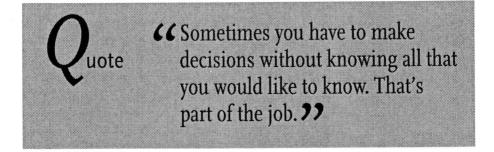

*Q*uote **"Sometimes you have to make decisions without knowing all that you would like to know. That's part of the job."**

Philanthropists

BROOKE ASTOR

BORN: 9/30/1902
DIED: 8/13/2007
OCCUPATION: Philanthropist and Writer

Nicknamed the "First Lady of Philanthropy," she was the daughter of a general when born in New Hampshire. She married as a teenager, then divorced in 1930. Her second marriage was to a stockbroker who died in 1952, but during the marriage she worked as an editor at *House and Garden* magazine. Her third marriage was in 1953 to Vincent Astor, part of the esteemed Astor family. He had great wealth. When he died in 1959, he left $60 million to her and $60 million for her to give to charity. She had great joy being driven around the city and making donations: to poor churches, barrios, tenements, boys' and girls' clubs, to landmarks and to homes for the elderly. She also gave generously to the Bronx Zoo, the Metropolitan Museum of Art and libraries. She gave her wealth to New York because so much of the Astor fortune had been made in real estate in the city. She ended up donating nearly $200 million. She was seen as a bridge from the Gilded Age to the Modern Age. For her generosity, she was awarded the Presidential Medal of Freedom in 1998.

BIO BITS

- A baby elephant at The Bronx Zoo was named "Astor" in her honor.
- She died at the age of 105.
- She wrote four books over her lifetime, including *Footprints: An Autobiography*.

Quote **"Power is the ability to do good things for others."**

PIERRE TOUSSAINT
BORN: 6/27/1766
DIED: 6/30/1853
OCCUPATION: Philanthropist

He was born a slave on a Haitian plantation and might someday be canonized as a saint by the Catholic Church. Toussaint was raised as a house slave in Haiti, was brought to NYC at age 21 by his owners who made him apprentice as a hairdresser. He was highly regarded by the elite and earned good money, much of which he was allowed to keep. He was freed at age 41 in 1807. Smart and articulate, he wrote volumes of letters. He married and he and his wife began a life of charitable acts. He provided money and food for orphans and the poor. He owned a house on Franklin Street and used it to foster orphans. He helped boys learn trades and get jobs. He organized a credit bureau and employment agency. He raised money for immigrants on which to live. He nursed patients with cholera and yellow fever during epidemics. He helped finance the St. Vincent de Paul School on Canal Street, the city's first Catholic school for black children. He was a spiritual and financial force in building St. Patrick's Old Cathedral on Mulberry Street.

BIO BITS
- He attended mass daily for 66 years at St. Peter's in New York.
- He is two steps away from being declared a saint by the Catholic Church.
- He is buried in St. Patrick's Old Cathedral Cemetery on Mulberry Street.

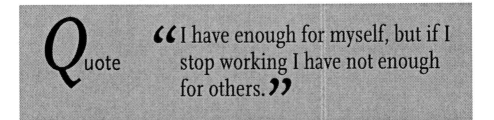

Quote **"I have enough for myself, but if I stop working I have not enough for others."**

ABBY ALDRICH ROCKEFELLER

BORN: 10/26/1874
DIED: 4/5/1948
OCCUPATION: Philanthropist

She helped establish modern art as we know it. Her father was a bookkeeper in Rhode Island who rose to become a U.S. senator. She was an outgoing and charming girl and received an excellent education. She sailed overseas and became very learned in art. In 1894 she met John D. Rockefeller, who was enormously wealthy due to his family's Standard Oil Company fortune. They married seven years later and had six children. He was shy, she was outgoing. He depended on her tremendously. She helped soften the harsh public opinion against him through public service and philanthropy. She served on the board of the YWCA for years and worked for the Red Cross in WWI. She helped provide safe housing for women in NYC. She was vital to the founding of the Museum of Modern Art (MoMA) in 1929. Through her gifts and leadership, MoMA has grown into one of the most important museums in the world. She gave many paintings, drawings and sculptures from her own collection, as well as contributions of money and land from the Rockefeller family to maintain MoMA.

BIO BITS

- She was a primary force behind the restoration of Colonial Williamsburg.
- She was a descendent of the Mayflower Pilgrims.
- Her early education came from Quaker governesses.

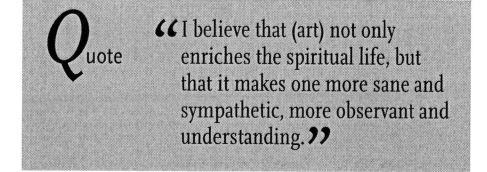

Quote **"I believe that (art) not only enriches the spiritual life, but that it makes one more sane and sympathetic, more observant and understanding."**

PEGGY GUGGENHEIM
BORN: 8/26/1898
DIED: 12/23/1979
OCCUPATION: Philanthropist and Arts Patron

Her father went down with the Titanic in 1912 but that didn't sink her incredible life in art. Born into a wealthy Jewish family, she inherited a fortune at age 21 (valued today at over $30 million). In 1920 she moved from New York to Paris, which had a vibrant community of artists. They included Picasso, Chagall, Modigliani, Ernst, as well as writers Hemingway and Fitzgerald. She made countless friends and became an art collector in the 1930s. She is noted for supporting modern artists by buying their works as often as one per day. As WWII broke out and the Germans approached Paris, Guggenheim slipped to the south of France with hundreds of works of art. She escaped to the U.S. and continued promoting modern art. After WWII she settled in Venice and installed a famous gallery in her home. Before her death, she donated her art collection to the Guggenheim Museum, named for a famous uncle. The Guggenheim Museum, designed by Frank Lloyd Wright and built at Fifth Avenue and 89th Street, holds much of her amazing collection of art works.

BIO BITS
- She was tutored at home and had a lonely, restricted childhood.
- She was a friend of poor artists in Paris, many living in the Montparnasse quarter.
- She supported many artists and sent a monthly check to writer Djuna Barnes for 50 years.

*Q*uote **❝I took advice from none but the best. I listened, how I listened! That's how I finally became my own expert.❞**

ALFRED T. WHITE
BORN: 5/28/1846
DIED: 1/29/1921
OCCUPATION: Philanthropist and Social Reformer

His goal was to provide affordable and dignified housing for the poor and that's what he built. Born the son of a wealthy importer, White earned an engineering degree at Rensselaer Polytech in 1865. He came back to work in the family business. He then volunteered in settlements for immigrants and saw their terrible living conditions. He set out to stop needless deaths through better housing. He built a new kind of tenement, the most advanced in the world, with private toilets,  sunny rooms, balconies and parks. He tried to create small, peaceful villages. He first housed 1,000 families, then created more and better. He started a kindergarten and became a leader in preschool education. He is credited with cutting infant mortality in Brooklyn in half as a member of the Children's Aid Society and founder of the Brooklyn Society for the Prevention of Cruelty to Children and the Brooklyn Bureau of Charities. He later became a major supporter of the Hampton and Tuskegee Institutes, and he endowed a chair to teach social ethics at Harvard.

BIO BITS
- His wife was a granddaughter of Seth Low and taught at a settlement school.
- He assisted building the Brooklyn Botanic Garden and funded them greatly.
- He died when he fell through thin ice while ice skating and drowned.

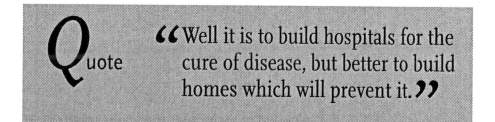

Quote

“Well it is to build hospitals for the cure of disease, but better to build homes which will prevent it.”

Artists

68

ANDY WARHOL
BORN: 8/6/1928
DIED: 2/22/1987
OCCUPATION: Artist

He was the son of a Pittsburgh construction worker who became one of the most influential artists in history. When Warhol was in bed at the age of eight with a disease, his mother gave him a drawing pad. After that art became his obsession. At nine his mom gave him a movie camera and he made his own movies. He was ceaselessly creative. He moved to New York in 1949 to become a commercial artist and was hugely successful through the 1950s, often working for *Glamour* magazine. In 1961 he started producing "pop art" (popular art), which was based on items like Campbell's soup cans. He parodied celebrities like Marilyn Monroe and Elvis Presley. He made a fortune while relishing being a celebrity himself. His fame soared and he was at the center of the New York's "It Scene." He opened his own art studio in 1964, called The Factory, and many avant-garde artists hung out there. He made art fun, basing it on everyday items, or famous people, and mixing it with wild, repetitive colors. He died after complications from gallbladder surgery in NYC.

BIO BITS

- In 2013 his work *Silver Car Crash* sold for $105.4 million at auction.
- He was shot by an actress friend in 1968 because she said he kept her script.
- He made a film called *Empire* in 1964 that was eight hours of a camera staring at the Empire State Building.

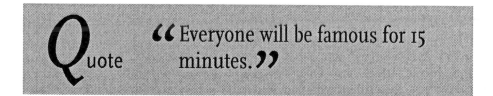

Quote **"Everyone will be famous for 15 minutes."**

69

LANGSTON HUGHES
BORN: 5/1/1902
DIED: 5/22/1967
OCCUPATION: Poet, Playwright, Cultural Leader

Two of his great-grandparents were black slaves, and two were white slave-owners (one Jewish). He grew up to be a leader of the Harlem Renaissance. His grandmother was one of the first women to attend Oberlin College. His father deserted the family so he was raised by his mom and grandmother in Kansas, Illinois and Ohio. In high school he was elected class poet, wrote for the school paper, and wrote stories and plays. He went to Columbia to study engineering but left early to concentrate on writing. He was at the forefront of an art form titled, "Jazz Poetry." He traveled the world. His poems were published throughout the 1920s and in 1934 a book of short stories was published. In 1935 he received a Guggenheim Fellowship. He became active in theatre and co-wrote the screenplay for the musical, *Way Down South*. Though he traveled widely, Harlem was his touchstone and nourished his soul, at the same time he nourished the souls of others. He celebrated black pride and influenced the writing of James Baldwin and Alice Walker, among others.

BIO BITS
- He graduated from Lincoln University and was a classmate of the first African-American Supreme Court Justice Thurgood Marshall.
- NYC has given landmark status to his home at 20 E. 127th Street.
- His ashes are interred in Harlem below the foyer of the Schomburg Center for Research in Black Culture.

*Q*uote **"Hold fast to dreams, for if dreams die, life is a broken-winged bird that cannot fly."**

AGNES DE MILLE
BORN: 9/18/1905
DIED: 10/7/1993
OCCUPATION: Choreographer and Dancer

She was told when she was young that she wasn't pretty enough to be an actress so she dove into dance. Then she was told she didn't have a dancer's body and she'd never succeed at dance! She graduated from UCLA. Her uncle, the famous film director Cecil B. DeMille (yes, they spell their names differently), got her a job in dance but the chief choreographer on the film fired her. Her breakout came in 1942 while choreographing *Rodeo* by Aaron Copland; her dance creation was so powerful that it is still seen in repertoires today. *Rodeo* led to the chance to choreograph *Oklahoma!* in 1943. It was a smashing success and her "Dream Ballet" is considered one of the best dances ever. De Mille was successful because she loved acting and put acting on display in her dances. Her choreography explored emotions while still enhancing the plot. One could see a character's inner struggles and not just a pretty dancing body. She went on to choreograph more than a dozen musicals, including *Carousel* and *Brigadoon*. She spoke widely to support dance in America, including testifying before Congress.

BIO BITS
- She won a Tony Award in 1947 for choreographing *Brigadoon*.
- Her secret hobbies were collecting porcelain and researching the history of clothes, at which she was reportedly an expert.
- She wrote over a dozen books, nearly all of them about dance.

*Q*uote **"To dance is to be out of yourself. Larger, more beautiful, more powerful."**

JERRY SEINFELD
BORN: 4/29/1954
DIED: —
OCCUPATION: Comedian, Actor, Producer

His father was a sign-maker and closet comedian so Jerry got his start at home. Born in Brooklyn, at the age of eight he was already trying to perfect his comedy routine. He watched TV constantly to see what made comedians funny. After graduating from Queens College, he performed at standup clubs. His reputation grew until he appeared on *The Tonight Show* in 1981. He improved his act throughout the 1980s and was given a chance to create his own series in 1988 by NBC, called *Seinfeld*. The series ran nine seasons and is considered among TV's greatest shows. Reruns can be found daily on stations across the globe. *Seinfeld* is based in NYC and it shows his love for New Yorkers as he mines humor from the most mundane city situations. Seinfield has given away millions of dollars to the needy, and his wife started a charity called Baby Buggy to assist poor women and children in their struggles. Few people have given so much pleasure to others—and based it on people you see on the street every day. He is also a successful theatre director.

BIO BITS
- Comedy Central named him the twelfth greatest comedian of all time.
- He did volunteer work in Kibbutz Sa'ar in Israel at age 16.
- He said *Seinfeld* was influenced by The Abbot and Costello Show that ran on TV in the 1950s.

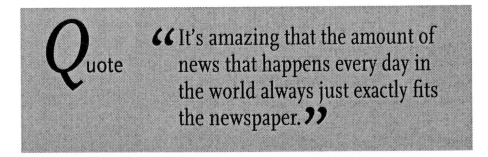

Quote **"It's amazing that the amount of news that happens every day in the world always just exactly fits the newspaper."**

ALICE AUSTEN
BORN: 3/17/1866
DIED: 6/9/1952
OCCUPATION: Photographer

Her father abandoned the family before she was born, yet she went on to become a famous photographer. After Austen's birth in Staten Island, her mother returned to her parent's home. At age 10 her uncle brought home a camera. It changed her forever. A closet was converted to a darkroom and for over 40 years she processed 8,000 photographs there. She met Gertrude Tate (a kindergarten teacher from Brooklyn) in 1899 and they became lifelong partners. Austen's photos of Staten Island society and the Lower East Side's poor are stunning. She was able to live on funds from her grandfather but after the Wall Street Crash of 1929, her finances were wiped out. She had to sell everything. In 1945 her house was confiscated by a bank and she sold all she had for $600 and moved out. Austen gave her photos to the Staten Island Historical Society, was declared a pauper, and in 1950 moved to a poorhouse called "The Farm Colony" on Staten Island. Her photos were rediscovered and soon afterward supporters raised $4,000 to send her to a nursing home.

BIO BITS
- She is buried in Moravian Cemetery in New Dorp, Staten Island.
- Alice Austen day is held on October 9th every year in celebration of her life.
- "Clear Comfort," Austen's ancestral home, still stands on Staten Island and in 1976 was made a national landmark.

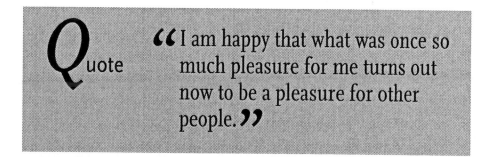

*Q*uote **❝ I am happy that what was once so much pleasure for me turns out now to be a pleasure for other people. ❞**

JIM HENSON
BORN: 9/24/1936
DIED: 5/16/1990
OCCUPATION: Puppeteer and Artist

The arrival of his family's first TV was the biggest event of his life. He watched a lot of it, then went on to change TV forever. He loved puppets as a boy. He was a huge fan of Kukla, Fran and Ollie on television. He was raised in the Christian Scientist faith and grew up in Maryland. At age 18 he already had puppet skills and was hired by a local TV show to perform. For seven years he experimented with puppets and created his own that expressed emotion. He made money doing commercials. He moved to NYC in 1963 with his company, Muppets, Inc. In 1969 Henson was invited to join *Sesame Street*. Through the 1970s and beyond, the Muppets and *Sesame Street* would be seen by vast numbers of children who laughed and learned through the Muppets. Henson made movies, had a TV show in the evening at one point, and won countless awards. He created the Jim Henson Foundation to develop puppetry as an art form. Kermit, Elmo, Miss Piggy, Bert and Ernie, Oscar and Cookie Monster are as recognizable today as any star in Hollywood. He died from a bacterial infection.

BIO BITS
- His dad worked for the United States Department of Agriculture.
- He sang the song, "Rainbow Connection," and it was nominated for an Academy Award.
- He collaborated with George Lucas on *Labyrinth*, a film considered a cult classic.

*Q*uote **❝ If you care about what you do and work hard at it, there isn't anything you can't do if you want to. ❞**

LOUIS COMFORT TIFFANY
BORN: 2/18/1848
DIED: 1/17/1933
OCCUPATION: Artist and Entrepreneur

He had his heart set on being an artist, though his father sent him to a military academy. Born in NYC, Louis was the son of the founder of the Tiffany Jewelry Company. He studied painting but it was making art from glass that inspired him. In 1875 he worked for a few Brooklyn glasshouses, then opened his own glass-making business. His genius led him to design glass for Mark Twain's house in Hartford, and President Chester Arthur had him redesign the White House. In 1885 he opened the Tiffany Glass Company, where he  created shimmering works by using opalescent, colorful glass. He used his own techniques with copper foil to manufacture windows and lamps. In 1893 he built a factory in Queens and employed as many as 300 artisans. Lamps created there wowed the World's Fair in Chicago in 1893. Then in 1900 he won a gold medal at the Paris Exposition. In 1902 he became the first design director for Tiffany & Co., the jewelry company that his father founded. His spectacular windows can still be seen in churches and buildings throughout NYC.

BIO BITS
- He is buried in Green-Wood Cemetery in Brooklyn.
- He fabricated and installed a huge, glass curtain in Mexico City for the Palacio de Bellas Artes that is a masterpiece of artistic design.
- He is considered the greatest force of the *Art Nouveau* style.

Quote **" Color is to the eye what music is to the ear. "**

75

RALPH ELLISON
BORN: 3/1/1913
DIED: 4/16/1994
OCCUPATION: Novelist, Essayist, Scholar

His father died when he was three after an ice block fell and filled his abdomen with ice shards. He had to support this family growing up so he worked as a bus-boy, shoe shiner and hotel waiter. He studied music and became a bandmaster. He got into the prestigious Tuskegee Institute in Alabama by playing the trumpet, then hopped on freight trains to get there. He played in the band and worked in the school library. He read the world's best writers, which gave him a feeling for superb literature. He moved to Harlem in 1936 before graduating and became part of the cultural scene. He met great African-American writers Langston Hughes and Richard Wright. They advised him and he collaborated with them. His short stories and book reviews began to be frequently published. After WWII, he poured himself into writing and finished *Invisible Man*, his masterpiece, in 1952. A year later it won the National Book Award for Fiction. He became world renowned. He traveled widely and was sought after as a lecturer for his insights into literature and society.

BIO BITS
- His father named him Ralph Waldo Ellison after Ralph Waldo Emerson.
- In 1958 he took a job teaching American and Russian literature at Bard College.
- He is interred at Trinity Church Cemetery in Washington Heights.

Quote **"**I am an invisible man ... I am invisible, understand, simply because people refuse to see me.**"**

MARTIN SCORSESE
BORN: 11/17/1942
DIED: —
OCCUPATION: Film Director, Producer, Actor

Who knew that asthma would have such an impact? Scorsese was born in Queens then moved to Little Italy before starting school. Asthma prevented him from playing sports so he spent his free time watching TV. He fell in love with movies. Even at age eight, he drew storyboards for films that he wanted to make. A short film he created earned him a $500 scholarship to New York University. After graduating with an MFA, he made his first full-length film in 1968 called, *Who's That Knocking at My Door?* That wasn't released until 10 years later when his other films made him famous. In 1973 Scorsese directed *Mean Streets*, which launched his career. During his 50+ year career, he has earned eight Best Director nominations (second most ever) and won for *The Departed* in 2006. His films often have troubled leading characters in a dangerous world. He has had more influence on young directors than any other person and his films *Taxi Driver* and *Raging Bull*, which reflect an intense New York experience, are considered among cinema's greatest achievements.

BIO BITS

- Both of his parents worked in New York City's garment district.
- He was raised devoutly Catholic and considered becoming a priest.
- He has been married five times, first to the influential writer of *The Artist's Way*, Julia Cameron.

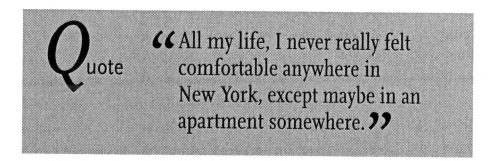

Quote ❝All my life, I never really felt comfortable anywhere in New York, except maybe in an apartment somewhere.❞

77

MARTHA GRAHAM
BORN: 5/11/1894
DIED: 4/1/1991
OCCUPATION: Choreographer and Dancer

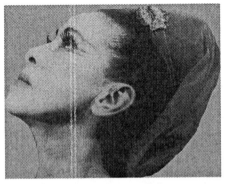

She saw her first dance performance at age 14 and it changed her forever. Graham went on to become a leader of Modern Dance. She studied dance in California, then taught it until 1925. She traveled to New York and was hired at the Eastman School of Music in Rochester. In 1926 she moved to NYC and formed the Martha Graham Center of Contemporary Dance. Her "Modern Dance" dropped the strict rules of ballet in favor of free movement and physical expression and improvisation. Through her choreography she told stories about what was happening around her, such as the Great Depression and Spanish Civil War. A popular dance she created was about the myth, Clytemnestra. She was invited by Hitler to dance in Germany in 1936 but declined. The Roosevelts asked her to dance at the White House so she became the first dancer to perform there. Her studio in NYC was a mecca for dance. Her impact is similar to what Picasso did for art, Stravinski for music, and Frank Lloyd Wright for architecture. She choreographed her final dance at the age of 95.

BIO BITS
- The Martha Graham Dance Company is the oldest dance company in America.
- She was named the "Dancer of the Century" by *Time* magazine in 1998.
- Her father was a practitioner of an early form of psychiatry.

Quote **"What the people in the world think of you is really none of your business."**

EUGENE O'NEILL

BORN: 10/16/1888
DIED: 11/27/1953
OCCUPATION: Playwright

He is considered the "Father of Realism" for the American stage. O'Neill was born in Times Square. His father was an Irish immigrant actor and an alcoholic who often went on tour, causing O'Neill to be boarded at a Catholic school in the Bronx. His mother became a drug addict. As a boy, he lost himself in books. He went to Princeton but was thrown out—possibly because he threw a beer bottle into the window of college president Woodrow Wilson. He spent a few years as a sailor, then went to Harvard, but quit. He started seriously writing plays after that, many of which were performed in Greenwich Village. In 1920, *Beyond the Horizon* appeared on Broadway and won the Pulitzer Prize. He had a string of theatre successes. In 1936 he received the Nobel Prize for Literature. His most famous play, among the finest ever in theatre, is *A Long Day's Journey Into Night*. It was finished in 1942 but not published until 1956. It then appeared on Broadway and won the Tony Award for Best Play. The play is about his own family's delusions and addictions.

BIO BITS

- He had tuberculosis at age 22 and recovered at a sanatorium for two years.
- He wrote only one comedy that is widely known: *Ah, Wilderness!*
- His daughter, Oona, married actor Charlie Chaplin and they had eight children.

*Q*uote **"God gave us mouths that close and ears that don't . . . that should tell us something."**

BILLIE HOLIDAY

BORN: 4/7/1915
DIED: 7/17/1959
OCCUPATION: Singer

She was born Eleanora Fagan and got the nickname "Lady Day" but it was Billie Holiday who became the famous jazz singer. Her parents were unmarried teens in Philadelphia. Her father left the family to pursue his own jazz career. Holiday went to Baltimore to be raised by her aunts. At age nine she was sent to a reform school for truancy. Her mom and she moved to Harlem in 1929, then were sent to prison for prostitution. When released, Holiday sang in Harlem nightclubs. Her first hit record came at age 17. She was sought after for her unique jazz phrasing. In 1937 she sang with big bands like Count Basie and Artie Shaw. Her popularity grew through the 1930s and 40s while she made records and sang in clubs. From 1945–47, she made $250,000. Then she went to prison for drug use. Within a year she was back and played to a sold-out Carnegie Hall and Broadway shows. She was again arrested for drugs and had health problems due to drug and alcohol use. She was popular in the 1950s but her reputation was badly damaged. She died with 70¢ in the bank.

BIO BITS

- She has five singles and one album in the Grammy Hall of Fame.
- Her albums have won four Grammy Awards for Best Historical Album since 1980.
- She is buried in Saint Raymond's Cemetery in the Bronx.

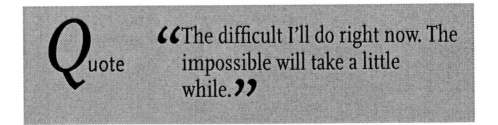

Quote **"The difficult I'll do right now. The impossible will take a little while."**

THE MARX BROTHERS
BORN: 1887–1901
DIED: 1961–1979
OCCUPATION: Entertainers

These Manhattan-born brothers are considered the greatest comedy act of the 20th Century. (Real names: Leonard, Adolph, Julius, Milton, and Herbert Marx.) Sons of Jewish immigrants, their dad was a tailor and they lived on the Upper East Side. As children, they were encouraged to play instruments and sing. Groucho sang in vaudeville in 1905, then over time his brothers joined him. Their singing evolved until finally, in 1912, they made their first performance in Marx Brothers' style: each brother playing a unique character. After vaudeville, they became a hit on Broadway in the 1920s with their own plays. In 1929 their shows began to be filmed and were huge successes. Their absurdist humor and quick wit tickled America's funny bone. They appeared on the cover of *Time* magazine in 1932. In 1933 their movie, *Duck Soup*, would go on to be considered one of the best 100 films ever. They continued making movies until 1949 for a total of 15 films. Thereafter, the brothers became successful in business and Groucho flourished in a TV career.

BIO BITS
- Their mother, Minnie, was the boys' manager and a tough negotiator.
- Harpo played six instruments and got his name from his incredible harp playing.
- Zeppo became a multi-millionaire through his engineering business.

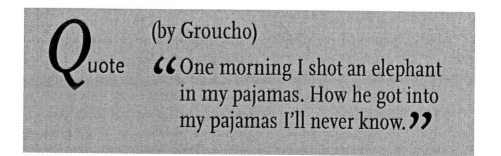

Quote **(by Groucho)**
❝One morning I shot an elephant in my pajamas. How he got into my pajamas I'll never know.❞

JAMES BALDWIN
BORN: 8/2/1924
DIED: 12/1/1987
OCCUPATION: Novelist and Activist

His father was a drug addict. His mother left his father and moved to Harlem before James was born. When his mother remarried the new family was dirt poor, so James had to care for his young siblings. He attended P.S. 24 on 128th Street. He went to DeWitt Clinton High School in the Bronx and worked on the school magazine. He worked in a sweatshop on Canal Street. Near there, he was encouraged to write by painter Beauford Delaney. Surrounded by racism, and hating it, he moved to Paris in 1948. His writing began to be published in anthologies. In 1953 his first novel, *Go Tell It On the Mountain*, was published, then his essays, *Notes of a Native Son*, in 1955. In 1956 his second novel, *Giovanni's Room*, was published. These books are considered classics. Though his permanent home was in Europe, he often returned to America to write for magazines about the civil rights movement. In the 1950s and 60s, he traveled to Montgomery and Selma, Alabama. He also marched in Washington, D.C. He was one of history's great civil rights writers and participants.

BIO BITS
- In 1944 his roommate was actor Marlon Barndo.
- His first published work appeared in *The Nation* magazine in 1947.
- When younger, he was a junior minister and preached from the pulpit with great success.

*Q*uote **"The world is before you and you need not take it or leave it as it was when you came in."**

MARGARET BOURKE-WHITE
BORN: 6/14/1904
DIED: 8/27/1971
OCCUPATION: Photographer

Her mother was Catholic and her father Jewish and she was born in the Bronx. Her father was an engineer, her mother a progressive. She went to Columbia, then left and in time graduated from Cornell in 1927. Bourke-White learned photography and came to NYC when Henry Luce offered her work in 1929. She was sent to Germany and Russia and the photos she took made her famous. She became *Life*'s first female staff photographer in 1936. She began shooting photos of social problems like the conditions of the poor and blacks. She went to Europe to document the rise of Hitler and was shocked by the anti-Semitism. She was in the Soviet Union in 1941 when Germany attacked and she took photos. She was in a boat that was torpedoed and went on a bombing mission. She was with General Patton as his troops crossed Germany. She took photos of the liberation of the Buchenwald concentration camp. She went to India to photograph Ghandi and Hindus and Muslims, then went to South Africa to document apartheid. Few have blended courage and art so spectacularly.

BIO BITS
- While in Russia, she photographed Joseph Stalin wearing a rare smile.
- In WWII she was repeatedly shot at while traveling with U.S. troops in Italy.
- She photographed Ghandi a few hours before his assassination in 1948.

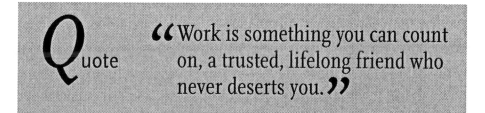

*Q*uote **"Work is something you can count on, a trusted, lifelong friend who never deserts you."**

GEORGE BALANCHINE

BORN: 1/22/1904
DIED: 4/30/1983
OCCUPATION: Choreographer

He wasn't interested in ballet as a child but was pushed into it. He then went on to become the greatest choreographer of modern ballet. Balanchine was born in St. Petersburg, Russia. After an audition at age nine, he was sent to the Imperial Ballet School. He became a member of a dance company and designed ballets as a teen. In 1924 he escaped Communist Russia for Paris. He joined the famous Ballets Russes and choreographed for composers such as Stravinsky, Debussy and Ravel. Sets and costumes were designed by Picasso and Matisse. He moved to NYC in 1934 and organized the American Ballet, part of the Metropolitan Opera. He also choreographed 20 Broadway shows. In 1946 the basis for the New York City Ballet was launched. This became his ballet company and he prolifically designed dances that came to be performed by ballet companies worldwide. His version of *The Nutcracker* has been performed in New York every year since 1955. He revolutionized American dance through his 400 choreographed works and by establishing the New York City Ballet.

BIO BITS

- He married and divorced five times and all his wives were dancers.
- A serious knee injury around 1930 led him to abandon a career as a dancer.
- He is interred at Oakland Cemetery in Sag Harbor on Long Island.

Quote

" First comes the sweat. Then comes the beauty if you're lucky and have said your prayers. "

GEORGE GERSHWIN
BORN: 9/26/1898
DIED: 7/11/1937
OCCUPATION: Composer and Pianist

He cared nothing for music as a boy, then ended up changing the musical world. He was born on Snediker Avenue in Brooklyn, the son of poor Jews from Russia. Gershwin heard a friend's violin recital at age 10 and then decided he wanted to be a pianist more than anything. He devoted himself to it day and night. He got a job on Tin Pan Alley and sat at a piano playing for passersby so that they would buy the sheet music he played. For that he was paid $15 per week. He recorded and sold his own piano rolls. He composed and his first big hit in 1919 was *Swanee*. He then collaborated on musicals and his fame grew. In the 1920s his name was in lights over Broadway for musicals like, *Lady Be Good, Funny Face* and *Strike Up the Band!* He won the Pulitzer Prize in 1931 for *Of Thee I Sing.* But it was *Porgy and Bess* (his unsurpassed African-American opera), *Rhapsody in Blue* and *An American in Paris* that assured his fame as a composer. He died at age 38 of a brain tumor. America was devastated. Had Gershwin lived a long life, his musical genius would have ranked him with Mozart.

BIO BITS
- His parents moved to New York because of anti-Jewish sentiment in Russia.
- A theater is named after him, The Gershwin, on Broadway.
- His brother, Ira, was a famous lyricist and wrote the words for most of the music that he composed.

*Q*uote **"Writing music is not so much inspiration as hard work."**

Writers and Journalists

NELLIE BLY

BORN: 5/5/1864
DIED: 1/27/1922
OCCUPATION: Writer and Entrepreneur

She was among the earliest undercover reporters. Born outside of Pittsburgh, her birth name was Elizabeth Jane Cochran. Her father immigrated from Ireland. She wrote so well at her school that she was offered a job writing for a newspaper at age 17. She chose the pen name "Nellie Bly." She wrote articles about women working in factories. At age 21 she went to Mexico for six months as a foreign correspondent. She then moved to NYC in 1887 to be a reporter but after four months had no work and was broke. In desperation she took a job reporting on hospital conditions in a lunatic asylum and pretended to be insane. She stayed for 10 days. Her report on the horrible conditions brought her enormous fame. Then she made an incredible 72-day trip around the world and reported on it for a newspaper. She married a millionaire in 1895 and left journalism to become president of the Iron Clad Manufacturing Company. She created several inventions and was a leading industrialist. Thereafter she went back to reporting during WWI and on women's suffrage.

BIO BITS

- She went to boarding school but dropped out when her dad ran out of money.
- A Broadway musical in 1946 called *Nellie Bly* lasted 16 performances.
- She is buried in Woodlawn Cemetery in the Bronx.

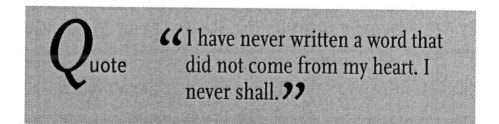

Quote **"I have never written a word that did not come from my heart. I never shall."**

ZORA NEALE HURSTON
BORN: 1/7/1891
DIED: 1/28/1960
OCCUPATION: Writer and Folklorist

Her parents were former slaves yet she went on to be one of America's great folklorists. She was born in Alabama, then at age three moved to Florida. Her mother died when she was 13. Troubled and expelled from boarding school, she made a living as a maid and singer. She attended Morgan College in Baltimore, then Howard University, then she got a scholarship to Barnard College in New York in 1925. She was the school's only African-American student. She lived in Harlem during the Harlem Renaissance of the 1920s. She did anthropological research in the American South, the Caribbean and Central America. She wrote extensively about the history and plight of the American Negro, published 4 novels, 50 short stories and plays, and essays. She exposed the roots of racism and celebrated black culture. However she had trouble finding consistent work. She was a freelance writer, then fired while a library worker in 1957 for being "too well educated." At the end of her life she was forced to work as a maid and accepted public assistance.

BIO BITS

- Her great work of fiction is *Their Eyes Were Watching God*.
- She was buried in an unmarked grave in Fort Pierce, Florida.
- Her Broadway playwriting debut came in 1932 for *The Great Day* but the show was cancelled after one performance.

*Q*uote **❝I will fight for my country, but I will not lie for her.❞**

JIMMY BRESLIN
BORN: 10/17/1930
DIED: 3/19/2017
OCCUPATION: Reporter

He didn't get to be one of New York's most popular newspaper reporters for nothin'. Breslin was widely read and his best pieces were about common people, like the "regular guy" who dug the grave for President Kennedy. Born in Queens, he was only four when his father walked out of the house one night and never returned. He was raised by his mother. In high school he tried to write for the school newspaper but was turned down because they didn't think he was smart enough. At age 17 he got a job as a copyboy for the *Long Island Press*. That launched his career. When he finally began to report the news, he was more interested in talking to little people on the street than big shots. He wrote for papers and magazines in a down-to-earth style that readers loved. He is most famous for his involvement in the 1977 Son of Sam murders, where the murderer actually wrote to him before he was caught, and the murderer's letters were published in a newspaper. Breslin published more than 20 books and won the prestigious Pulitzer Prize for commentary.

BIO BITS
- He acted in a movie and received a Worst Performance by a Novelist award.
- He had his own TV show in 1986 and often interviewed poor New Yorkers.
- He was viciously attacked in 1970 in a restaurant, likely by the Mafia, for his writing about their criminal activities.

Quote   **"When you leave New York you ain't going anywhere."**

88

ADA LOUISE HUXTABLE
BORN: 3/14/1921
DIED: 1/7/2013
OCCUPATION: Writer and Architectural Critic

She won the first-ever Pulitzer Prize for criticism in 1970 and was a brilliant advocate for architectural preservation at *The New York Times*. Born in NYC, she grew up near 89th Street and walked everywhere. That led her to really get to know buildings. She studied museums, Grand Central Terminal and apartments. Her father was a doctor. She went to Hunter College and NYU. She was a display assistant at Bloomingdale's, then worked for MoMA from 1946–50. She was a Fulbright and Guggenheim Fellow. The *Times* noticed her articles about buildings and hired her as their first-ever architecture critic in 1963. She became only the second female writer to win a Pulitzer Prize in 1970. She defined the field and that led other papers to hire their own architectural critics. Her views were biting and her humor was sharp. She advocated preserving structures rather than building giant cement blocks all around New York. Above all, she wanted human dignity to be respected in the buildings erected in the city. Her commentary helped save many landmarks from demolition and generated civic pride.

BIO BITS
- After working for the *Times*, she became a critic for *The Wall Street Journal*.
- She wrote 11 books, including a biography of Frank Lloyd Wright in 2004.
- She received a MacArthur "genius" grant in 1981 and received $200,000 for the prestigious award.

Q uote **" New York, thy name is irreverence and hyperbole. And grandeur. "**

WALT WHITMAN
BORN: 5/31/1819
DIED: 3/26/1892
OCCUPATION: Poet and Humanist

Born on Long Island, he moved to Brooklyn at the age of four. At six, Marquis de Lafayette picked him up and kissed him on the cheek during a July 4th celebration. Whitman finished his schooling at age 11, then had to work to support his family. He had trouble finding work due to the Panic of 1837, then took a job as a typesetter in 1839 in Queens, then became editor of the *Brooklyn Eagle* from 1846–48. He wrote his masterpiece, *Leaves of Grass*, during the early 1850s and published it with his own money in 1855. Ralph Waldo Emerson gave it tremendous praise. Over the next 30+ years, Whitman continued to edit and expand *Leaves of Grass* as it reached wider audiences. The Civil War deeply affected him and he moved to Washington to work for the government and volunteer as a nurse for the wounded. His poem, "O Captain! My Captain!", written about Abraham Lincoln after his death, was nationally acclaimed. After the Civil War, his fame increased internationally. He moved to Camden, NJ and revised and published his poems until his death.

BIO BITS
- He self-published 795 copies of the first edition of *Leaves of Grass*.
- He enjoyed sunbathing in the nude and advocated an all-meat diet.
- He loved crossing from Manhattan to Brooklyn on a ferry and wrote of it.

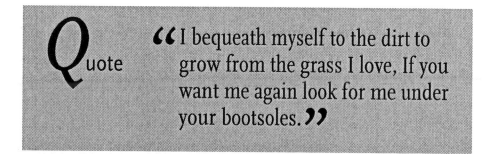

Quote **"**I bequeath myself to the dirt to grow from the grass I love, If you want me again look for me under your bootsoles.**"**

DOROTHY PARKER

BORN: 8/22/1893
DIED: 6/7/1967
OCCUPATION: Writer and Satirist

She had a horrible childhood. Her mother died when she was four. She said her father abused her. She loathed her stepmother, whom she called, "the housekeeper." She went to a Catholic school on 79th Street, though her father was Jewish. He died when she was 18. She earned her living playing piano for a dance studio, but she also wrote extensively and soon got a job at *Vogue*, then *Vanity Fair*. She became part of the famous Algonquin Round Table of writers. Her notoriety grew because of her caustic wit. She wrote for *The New Yorker* in 1925 and became celebrated for her short, satirical poetry. She wrote plays that appeared on Broadway, as well as wide-selling books of verse. Her short story, "Big Blonde," won the O. Henry Award in 1929. She moved to Hollywood, married, and earned $1,000 to $5,000 per week as a screenwriter. She also became an outspoken advocate for civil liberties and rights, which got her in trouble. She was blacklisted during the McCarthy Era and had trouble securing employment. She died in NYC while living at 23 E. 74th Street.

BIO BITS
- In her will, she bequeathed her estate to Dr. Martin Luther King, Jr.
- On her 99th birth anniversary, the Postal Service issued a stamp in her honor.
- She was born in a summer beach cottage in Long Branch, New Jersey.

Quote **"**Of course I talk to myself. I like a good speaker, and I appreciate an intelligent audience.**"**

AYN RAND

BORN: 2/2/1905
DIED: 3/6/1982
OCCUPATION: Writer and Philosopher

If you believe in self-sufficiency, you could be her disciple. Born in Russia, Rand was the daughter of a pharmicist. Lenin and the Bolsheviks confiscated her father's business after 1917 and the family nearly starved. She was then allowed to attend a university. She arrived in NYC in 1926 and cried at the beauty of the Manhattan skyline. She traveled to Hollywood to write for movies. In 1935 her play, *Night of January 16th*,  opened on Broadway. She finished her book, *The Fountainhead*, which took seven years to write, in 1943. It was a worldwide success and made into a film. She became an outspoken anti-Communist because of her past. She moved permanently to NYC in 1951 and worked on her greatest book, *Atlas Shrugged*, published in 1957. It advocated her philosophy of Objectivism, which states that the moral purpose of a life is to pursue happiness and rational self-interest. She believed that individual rights and capitalism are essential to a free and flourishing society. She ended her life teaching her philosophy at many universities.

BIO BITS
- She smoked heavily and in 1974 underwent surgery for lung cancer.
- She became an American citizen in 1931, five years after arriving in the U.S.
- She began writing her first novel at the age of 10.

*Q*uote **"The man who lets a leader prescribe his course is a wreck being towed to the scrap heap."**

ISAAC ASIMOV
BORN: 1/2/1920
DIED: 4/6/1992
OCCUPATION: Writer and Futurist

This godfather of science fiction was born in Russia to a family that milled grain. They immigrated to Brooklyn when Asimov was three and spoke only Yiddish. His parents owned a series of candy stores with papers and magazines. He grew up reading those and from that grew his love of words. Science fiction became his addiction and he wrote his own stories at age 11. He graduated from Boys High School at 15, then went to college at a branch of Columbia in Brooklyn. His first three sci-fi stories appeared in 1939 in *Amazing Stories* and *Astounding*. Within two years he had published 32 stories. One of them, "Nightfall," is considered the greatest sci-fi story of all time. He got his M.A. and Ph.D. from Columbia. In WWII he served as a civilian in the navy for three years, then was drafted in 1945 and served nine months. He worked for Boston University in chemistry after 1948 but by that time he earned more from writing sci-fi than from BU. He moved to the Upper West Side in 1970 and lived there for the rest of his life.

BIO BITS
- He was afraid of flying and only flew in planes twice during his life.
- He wrote and edited more than 500 books and 90,000 letters and postcards.
- He wanted to own a candy store in a subway station so the trains would rumble by as he read.

*Q*uote **"Above all things, never think you're not good enough yourself... My belief is that in life people will take you at your own reckoning."**

Sports Figures

JACKIE ROBINSON
BORN: 1/31/1919
DIED: 10/24/1972
OCCUPATION: Baseball Player

One of sport's greatest heroes, he broke baseball's color line. His father was a Georgia sharecropper when he was born. They moved to California when he was one and he was raised by his mother. They were poor. Robinson had many athletic gifts. He was admitted to UCLA and became their first athlete to letter in four sports. He was drafted into the Army in 1942 and became a lieutenant in 1943. In 1945 he played baseball in the Negro Leagues for $400 a month. Branch Rickey signed him to a minor league contract in 1946 to play for the Montreal Royals. On April 15, 1947 he made his Major League debut with the Brooklyn Dodgers. There were 26,623 spectators and 14,000 were black. The color line was broken and soon other African Americans were integrated into baseball. The abuse Jackie received was dangerous and teams threatened to strike if he played, but he kept his cool and endured. In a 1947 poll he was chosen as the second most popular man in the country. He was Rookie of the Year in 1947 and MVP in 1949. He was admitted to baseball's Hall of Fame in 1962.

BIO BITS

- He was an All-Star for six straight seasons from 1949 to 1954.
- Baseball retired his number, 42, so that no other players are allowed to wear it.
- He was the first African-American TV analyst for Major League Baseball in 1965.

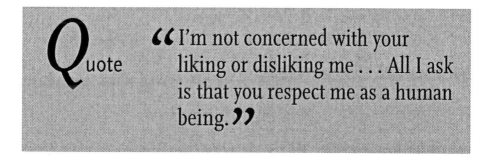

Quote **" I'm not concerned with your liking or disliking me . . . All I ask is that you respect me as a human being. "**

GEORGE HERMAN "BABE" RUTH
BORN: 2/6/1895
DIED: 8/16/1948
OCCUPATION: Baseball Player

He was arguably the greatest baseball player in history. Born in Baltimore, his parents had eight kids but only Babe and a sister survived. His dad owned a tavern and Babe constantly got into trouble. He wandered docks, chewed tobacco and broke laws. He was so difficult that his parents sent him to a Catholic home for boys at age seven. A monk, Brother Mathias, taught him baseball and Babe was a natural. By age 15 he caught the eyes of scouts. At 19 he was in the Majors. Boston signed him as a pitcher and he played with the Red Sox. In 1916 he pitched 13 scoreless innings in one game. In the greatest mistake Boston ever made, Babe was sold to the NY Yankees for $100,000 in 1919. Over the next 15 years, Babe led the Yanks to seven AL Championships and four World Series titles. He smashed every slugging record and hit 60 home runs in 1927, a record that stood for 34 years. Yankee Stadium, erected in 1923, was dubbed, "The House That Ruth Built." He had an extravagant personality but always found time to visit orphanages and help poor kids.

BIO BITS
- He was given the name "Babe" by other baseball players on his team because he was so young when he became a pro.
- He was also called "The Great Bambino" and "The Sultan of Swat" and "The King of Swing."
- He remained a practicing Catholic for his whole life.

*Q*uote **❝You can't beat the person who never gives up.❞**

VINCE LOMBARDI

BORN: 6/11/1913
DIED: 9/13/1970
OCCUPATION: Football Coach

The Super Bowl winner is given the Lombardi Trophy for it's named after football's greatest professional coach. Born in Sheepshead Bay, his grandparents were Italian immigrants. His dad owned a butcher shop in the Meatpacking District. He was an altar boy. He attended P.S. 206 and played organized football at 12 and got a scholarship to Fordham. He was selected assistant football coach for St. Cecilia's in NJ and there also taught Latin, Chemistry and Physics (paid less than $1,000 a year). His success led him to be an assistant coach at Fordham, then Army. In 1954 he took a coaching position for the New York Giants. In 1959 he was named the Green Bay Packers' head coach after the team had a 1-10-1 record in 1958. Lombardi demanded pure dedication and the Packers finished 7-5 in 1959. In 1960 he lost the championship to Philadelphia on the game's final drive. That's the only championship he ever lost. He went on to win five championships and two Super Bowls.

BIO BITS
- He coached the Redskins in 1969 for their first winning season in 14 years.
- His father went to church daily his whole life.
- If a player or coach showed sexual or racial discrimination, Lombardi fired them immediately.

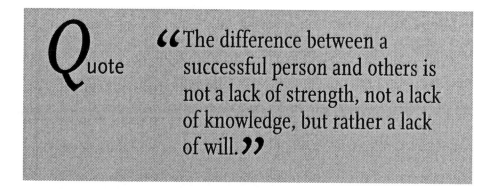

Quote

"The difference between a successful person and others is not a lack of strength, not a lack of knowledge, but rather a lack of will."

ALTHEA GIBSON
BORN: 8/25/1927
DIED: 9/28/2003
OCCUPATION: Tennis and Golf Player

This tennis great broke the female color line in sports. Her parents were sharecroppers when she was born. At age three Gibson and her family moved to Harlem. She went to public schools and, at age 12, was the NYC paddle tennis champion. Neighbors bought her a membership to a tennis club and she won her first tournament in 1941. She went on to win 10 straight women's tennis titles beginning in 1947. She received a full college scholarship to Florida A&M in 1949. She was the first African-American player invited to the U.S. National Championship in 1950 and the first at Wimbledon in 1951. She became the first African American to win a Grand Slam event at the French Open in 1956. In 1957 she won Wimbledon and got a ticker-tape parade in NYC. A month later she won the U.S. National Championship. In 1958 she repeated wins at Wimbledon and the U.S. National. She was named female athlete of the year by the Associated Press and was on the cover of *Time* and *Sports Illustrated*. She went on to a pro golfing career in 1964 at the age of 37.

BIO BITS
- Her early tennis lessons were at the Cosmopolitan Tennis Club in Harlem.
- As a singer and saxophonist, she was runner-up at an Apollo Theatre talent contest in 1943.
- She ended up winning 10 Grand Slam titles, including doubles.

Quote **"No matter what accomplishments you make, somebody helped you."**

JOE DIMAGGIO
BORN: 11/125/1914
DIED: 3/8/1999
OCCUPATION: Baseball Player

The 56-game hitting streak by this Yankee great will very likely never be topped. His parents were Sicilian immigrants. His dad went through Ellis Island. DiMaggio was born in California. His dad wanted him to be a fisherman but the smell of dead fish made him sick so he swore it off. He became a baseball legend instead. The Yankees got hold of him in 1936. In his rookie season he hit .323 with 29 home runs and the Yankees won the World Series. His grace, speed and desire were unmatched. Over the next 13 years, the Yankees won nine World Series with Joltin' Joe in centerfield. His greatest accomplishment came in 1941 when he hit in 56 straight games. He then spent three years in the Army during WWII (for which he was paid $21 a month). His parents were Italian and classified as "enemy aliens" so could not travel beyond five miles from home without a permit; his dad's fishing boat was also seized. After the war, DiMaggio returned to baseball and won the MVP award in 1947. He was elected to the Hall of Fame in 1955. In 1969 he was voted baseball's greatest living player.

BIO BITS
- He married Marilyn Monroe in 1954 and they divorced a year later.
- His brothers Vince and Dom were also major league centerfielders.
- He demanded combat duty in 1943 but the Army turned him down.

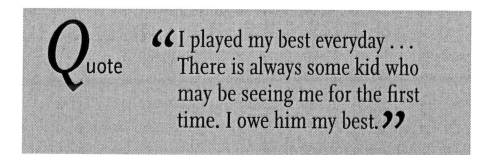

*Q*uote **"I played my best everyday... There is always some kid who may be seeing me for the first time. I owe him my best."**

98

JOE NAMATH

BORN: 5/31/1943
DIED: —
OCCUPATION: Football Player

He guaranteed the New York Jets would win the 1969 Super Bowl. Nobody believed him because the Jets were in the inferior American Football League, or AFL. But Namath drove the Jets to victory and football was changed forever. He was born near Pittsburgh and grew up poor. His dad was a steelworker and his grandpa came through Ellis Island. In high school he played football, baseball and basketball (and could dunk). Baseball teams offered him pro contracts but his mom wanted him to go to college so he went to the University of Alabama. He made them national college football champs in 1964. The Jets took him as their #1 pick in the draft. He was Rookie of the Year and became the first pro quarterback to throw 4,000 yards in 1967. His career peaked in 1969 in Super Bowl III when the Jets won 16–7 over the Baltimore Colts, led by QB Johnny Unitas. The press laughed at Namath when he guaranteed a win. He delivered and soon the AFL merged with the NFL to create the pro football league so popular today. He was elected to the Hall of Fame in 1985.

BIO BITS
- He got the nickname "Broadway Joe" from *Sports Illustrated* in 1965.
- He had a bad knee and sometimes it had to be drained at halftime during games.
- As an actor he has appeared in more that two dozen films and TV shows.

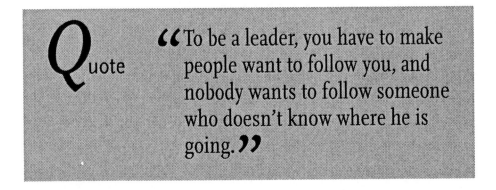

Quote **"To be a leader, you have to make people want to follow you, and nobody wants to follow someone who doesn't know where he is going."**

ARTHUR ASHE

BORN: 7/10/1943
DIED: 2/6/1993
OCCUPATION: Tennis Player and Humanitarian

He was the first great male African-American tennis player and a tremendous humanitarian. His childhood was tough. His mom died when he was six. His dad worried his son would grow up in trouble so timed his son's walk home from school to be sure he didn't mingle with riffraff. His dad was a caretaker for a public park with tennis courts so Ashe started playing tennis at seven.

He excelled. UCLA gave him a tennis scholarship. He became the NCAA singles and doubles champion. He joined the U.S. Army in 1966 and served for three years, yet still played tennis. He won the U.S. Open and Wimbledon. He played in segregated South Africa and was given a Zulu name: "Sipho" or "Gift From God." After retiring he became a role model. He protested apartheid in South Africa, pushed for all student athletes to receive better educations, and advocated that tennis be taught to poor children. He had brain surgery in 1988 and was infected with the HIV virus. He established the Arthur Ashe Foundation for the Defeat of AIDS. He died of the disease in 1993 and is renown for his compassion and dignity.

BIO BITS

- Bill Clinton awarded him the Presidential Medal of Freedom.
- When young his nickname was "Bones" because he was so skinny.
- He grew up in a caretaker cottage in one of Richmond, Virginia's parks.

*Q*uote **"From what we get, we can make a living; what we give, however, makes a life."**

KAREEM ABDUL-JABBAR

BORN: 4/16/1947

DIED: —

OCCUPATION: Basketball Player and Humanitarian

His birth name was Ferdinand Lewis Alcindor, Jr. and his dad was an NYC policeman. He was born in Harlem. By fifth grade he was six-feet tall and by eighth grade he could dunk. He went to Power Memorial Catholic High and led his team to 71 straight wins and three city titles. He choose UCLA for college. The NCAA changed their rules just for him to prohibit dunking because they feared Alcindor would dominate. He still dominated. UCLA won three national titles and he was named outstanding player three times. He was drafted by the Milwaukee Bucks and, in his second season, led them to their first and only NBA title. He was 7'2" and 230 pounds. His experiences with bigotry and his desire for justice led him to question his faith. He converted to Islam and in 1971 changed his name to Kareem Abdul-Jabbar. He moved to play for the Los Angeles Lakers in 1975 and over 15 seasons the Lakers reigned supreme. He leads the NBA in all-time points, rebounds, blocks and field-goal percentage. He is a six-time NBA champion and 19-time NBA all star.

BIO BITS

- His dad was a respected jazz trombone player.
- He started doing yoga in 1976 and credits it with his basketball longevity.
- He wrote many best-selling books and has acted in movies and TV shows.

Quote **"I think that the good and the great are only separated by the willingness to sacrifice."**

YOU MIGHT ALSO CONSIDER

There are millions of important New Yorkers, including teachers and fire-fighters and policemen. You might have a few New Yorkers of your own you wish were in this book. Below is a list of others who might have been included. Do some research on your own and find out who they are or make your own choices!

Bella Abzug   Public Servant
Elizabeth Cady Stanton   Suffragist and Activist
Joshua Lederberg   Biologist
Arthur Miller   Playwright
Lydia Kontos   Educator
Samuel Morse   Inventor
Belle and Henry Moskowitz   Activists
Daniel Patrick Moynihan   Public Servant
James Beard   Chef and Writer
James Weldon Johnson   Educator and Activist
Yogi Berra   Baseball Player
John J. Audubon   Artist
John Jacob Astor   Entrepreneur
Alvin Ailey   Choreographer
James Agee   Writer
Dorothy Day   Activist
William F. Buckely   Writer and Activist
Benjamin Cardozo   Jurist
Dominic Cuskern   Educator, Actor and Activist
Rocky Graziano   Boxer
Elizabeth Gurley Flynn   Feminist and Activist
Woody Gutherie   Singer and Songwriter
John Lennon   Singer and Songwriter
Jacob K. Javitz   Public Servant
Jack Kerouac   Writer and Activist
Ed Koch   Public Servant
Emma Lazarus   Writer and Activist
Pete Hamill   Journalist
Bernie Sanders   Public Servant

Spike Lee   Filmmaker
Norman Mailer   Writer and Activist
Gloria Steinem   Journalist and Activist
Bob Dylan   Musician and Poet
Bill De Blasio   Public servant
Norman Thomas   Activist
Daniel D. Tompkins   Public Servant
Edith Wharton   Writer
Walter Francis White   Activist
Betty Friedan   Activist
Richard Wright   Writer
Theodore S. Wright   Abolitionist and Activist
Joseph Seligman   Entrepreneur
Paul Simon   Singer and Songwriter
Alfred E. Smith   Public Servant
George Waring   Engineer and Public Servant
Mary Richmond   Activist
Paul Robeson   Actor and Activist
Bill Robinson (Bojangles)   Dancer
Henrietta Rodman   Educator and Feminist
Willie Mays   Baseball Player
Margaret Sanger   Nurse, Educator and Activist
Norman Rockwell   Painter
Sean Rice   Educator and Track Coach
Aaron Copland   Composer
Julia Ward Howe   Activist and Poet
Henry James   Writer
Herman Melville   Writer
Barbara Streisand   Singer
Sandy Koufax   Baseball Player
Verna Small   Preservationist
Jane Cunningham Croly   Journalist
Jane Grant   Journalist
Anna Ottendorfer   Journalist and Philanthropist
Tony Bennett   Singer and Philatropist
George Carlin   Comedian
Washington Irving   Writer
The Three Stooges   Comedians
Stephen Sondheim   Composer

PHOTO CREDITS

1. Wald: Harris & Ewing photograph, 1920, Library of Congress Prints and Photographs Division
2. Anthony: Francis Benjamin Johnson, photographer, 1900–06, Library of Congress Prints and Photographs Division
3. Foo: Public Domain photo prior to 1923, photographer unknown
4. Tappan: *Harpers Weekly*, 1873, Library of Congress Prints and Photographs Division
5. Gaston: Photographer unknown, photo courtesy of Board of Directors, Brownsville Heritage House, Inc.
6. Gompers: C. Frederiksen, photographer, 1904, San Juan, P.R., U.S. Copyright Office
7. Goldman: T. Kajiwara, photographer, copyright 1910, Library of Congress Rare Book and Special Collections Division, Paul Avrich Collection
8. Mathews: The New York Public Library Digital Collections, Schomburg Center for Research in Black Culture, Photographs and Prints Division: Astor, Lenox, and Tilden Foundation
9. Seixas: Anonymous impression from artist, source unknown
10. Schneiderman: Library of Congress, National Photo Company Collection, 1909–20
11. Riis: Library of Congress, George Grantham Bain Collection, Bain News Service staff photograph
12. Lowell: Public Domain Photo, 1898, *The National Cyclopedia of American Biography*
13. Pantoja: The Antonia Pantoja Papers. Archives of the Puerto Rican Diaspora, Centro de Estudios Puertorriqueños, Hunter College, CUNY, photographer unknown
14. Ovington: Library of Congress Prints and Photographs Division, 1910
15. Chisholm: Thomas O'Halloran, photographer, 1972, Library of Congress Prints and Photographs Division, *U.S. News and World Report* Magazine and Photograph Collection
16. Jay: Library of Congress, reproduction of painting by Joseph Wright, *Century Magazine*, 1889
17. La Guardia: Fred Palumbo, photographer, 1940, Library of Congress, *New York World-Telegram and Sun* Newspaper Photograph Collection

18. Hamilton: John Trumbull painter, 1790s, Public Domain, U.S. Federal Government
19. Ginsberg: Steve Petteway, photographer, 2006, Public Domain, collection of the Supreme Court of the United States
20. Ferraro: Rebecca Roth, photographer, 1998, Library of Congress Prints and Photographs Division
21. Corbin: From a sketch by Herbert Knotel, West Point Museum Art Collection, United States Military Academy
22. Giuliani: Jason Bedrick, photographer, 2006, released to the Public Domain
23. Hutchinson: unknown artist, National Women's Hall of Fame, source unknown
24. Bloomberg: Rubenstein, photographer, 2007, licensed under the Creative Commons agreement
25. Motley: John Botegga, photographer, 1965, Library of Congress Prints and Photographs Division, *New York World-Telegram and Sun* Newspaper Photograph Collection
26. Rohatyn: Photograph © Estate of Bernard Gotfryd
27. Moody: 1604 sketch by Wenceslaus Hollar, New England Historical Society
28. F. Roosevelt: Elias Goldensky, photographer, 1933, Library of Congress Prints and Photographs Division
29. E. Roosevelt: Library of Congress Prints and Photographs Division, 1933
30. T. Roosevelt: Pirie McDonald, photographer, 1915, Library of Congress Prints and Photographs Division, 1915
31. Trump: Joint Congressional Inauguration Committee, 2016, United States Congress
32. Perkins: Library of Congress Prints and Photographs Division, photo circa 1932
33. Cuomo: Kenneth C. Zirkel, photographer, 1987, released by permission to Public Domain
34. Kissinger: Thomas J. O'Halloran, photographer, 1975, Library of Congress Prints and Photographs Division
35. Gayle: H. J. Fields, photographer, New York Public Library Digital Collections
36. Jacobs: Phil Stanziola, photographer, 1961, Library of Congress Prints and Photographs Division, *New York World-Telegram and Sun* Newspaper Photograph Collection

37. Brady: New York Public Library Digital Collections, The Miriam and Ira D. Wallach Division of Art, Prints and Photographs: Print Collection

38. Onassis: Mark Shaw, photographer, 1961, Library of Congress Prints and Photographs Division

39. Wittenberg: Courtesy of the Greenwich Village Society for Historic Preservation

40. Schiff: Courtesy of the Franklin and Eleanor Roosevelt Institute, photographer unknown

41. Cooper: Mathew Brady, photographer, date unknown, Library of Congress

42. Walker: Scurlock Studio, 1905–19, Smithsonian Institution National Museum of American History

43. E. Roebling: Public Domain photograph, source Unknown. W. Roebling: New York Public Library Digital Collection

44. Steinbrenner: Public Domain photograph released by the New York Yankees and Major League Baseball

45. Papp: Billy Rose Theatre Division, The New York Public Library Digital Collections, 1960–1965, photographer unknown

46. Olmstead: Engraved by T. Johnson from a photograph by James Notman, *The Century* magazine, 1893, Library of Congress Prints and Photographs Division

47. Lebow: Public Domain photographer, New York Road Runners, licensed under the Creative Commons agreement

48. Vanderbilt: Mathew Brady, 1844–60, Library of Congress Prints and Photographs Division

49. Da Verrazzano: New York Public Library Digital Collections, The Miriam and Ira D. Wallach Division of Art, Prints and Photographs: Print Collection

50. Oppenheimer: 1944 photograph, U.S. Department of Energy, Office of Public Affairs

51. Minuit: Public Domain photographic reproduction of a work of art

52. Fulton: From a painting by Chappel in possession of Johnson, Wilson & Co. Publishers, Library of Congress Prints and Photographs Division

53. Ho: Provided by the Aaron Diamond AIDS Research Center for use

54. Stuyvesant: New York Public Library Digital Collections, The Miriam and Ira D. Wallach Division of Art, Prints and Photographs: Print Collection

55. Salk: Public Domain photograph, 1959, from SAS Scandinavian Airlines
56. McKinney-Steward: New York Public Library Digital Collections, Schomburg Center for Research in Black Culture, Photographs and Prints Division
57. Hudson: Speculative Portrait from *The Cyclopedia of Universal History*
58. Sagan: Public Domain photograph, 1980, U.S. National Aeronautics and Space Administration
59. Mead: Edward Lynch, photographer, Library of Congress Prints and Photographs Division, *New York World-Telegram and Sun* Newspaper Photograph Collection
60. Feynman: Public Domain photograph, 1943, United States Army
61. Tesla: Napoleon Sarony, photographer, 1890, Bain News Service, Library of Congress Prints and Photographs Division, George Grantham Bain Collection
62. Yellen: Official Portrait United States Federal Reserve, 2015
63. Astor: E. F. Foley, Photographer, 1922, entered into the Public Domain
64. Toussaint: Public Domain photograph, photographer unknown
65. Rockefeller: Public Domain photograph, photographer unknown
66. Guggenheim: Public Domain photograph, photographer unknown
67. White: Unsourced Public Domain photograph published before 1923, photographer unknown
68. Warhol: Jack Mitchell, photographer, 1966–77, Public Domain use allowed
69. Hughes: Carl Van Vechten, photographer, 1936, Library of Congress Prints and Photographs Division, Carl Van Vechten photograph collection
70. De Mille: Carl Van Vechten, photographer, 1941, Library of Congress Prints and Photographs Division, Carl Van Vechten photograph collection
71. Seinfield: Alan Light, photographer, 1997, released to the Public Domain by permission
72. Austen: Courtesy of The Staten Island Historical Societyand Historic Richmond Town
73. Henson: Alan Light, photographer, 1989, released to the Public Domain by permission
74. Tiffany: Photograph by Pach, 1908, Library of Congress Prints and Photographs Division

75. Ellison: United States Information Agency staff photographer, 1961
76. Scorsese: Georges Biard, photographer, 2009, at the Cannes Film Festival, released into the Public Domain by permission
77. Carl Van Vechten, photographer, 1961, Library of Congress Prints and Photographs Division, Carl Van Vechten photograph collection
78. Carl Van Vechten, photographer, 1933, Library of Congress Prints and Photographs Division, Carl Van Vechten photograph collection
79. Holiday: William P. Gottlieb, 1947, Library of Congress Music Division, in accordance with the wishes of William Gottlieb, the photographs in his collection have entered the Public Domain
80. Marx Brothers: Library of Congress Prints and Photographs Division, photographer unknown
81. Baldwin: Allan Warren, photographer, 1969, released into the Public Domain by permission
82. Bourke-White: Bureau of Industrial Service uncopyrighted photograph, 1955, Public Domain
83. Balachine: By Florida Memory—Portrait of Ringling Circus choreographer George Balachine: Sarasota, Florida
84. Gershwin: Mishkin 1935 from RR Auctions, entered into Public Domain without copyright registration
85. Bly: H. J. Myers, photographer, 1890, Library of Congress Prints and Photographs Division
86. Hurston: Library of Congress 1935–43, entered into Public Domain without copyright registration
87. Breslin: David Shankbone, 2008, released into the Public Domain by permission
88. Huxtable: Lynn Gilbert, photographer, 1981, licensed under the Creative Commons agreement
89. Whitman: George C. Cox, photographer, 1887, Library of Congress Prints and Photographs Division, Feinberg-Whitman Collection
90. Parker: Photo in the Public Domain, prior to 1923, unknown photographer
91. Rand: USSR passport photo 1925, Public Domain
92. Asimov: Phillip Leonian, photographer, pre-1959, Library of Congress Prints and Photographs Division, *New York World-Telegram and Sun* Newspaper Photograph Collection
93. Robinson: Bob Sandberg, photographer, 1954, Library of Congress Prints and Photographs Division, *LOOK* Magazine Photograph Collection, released by permission of Cowles Communications, Inc.

94. Ruth: Irwin, La Broad, & Pudlin Studio, 1920, Library of Congress Prints and Photographs Division
95. Lombardi: Photographer unknown 1967, Library of Congress Prints and Photographs Division, *New York World-Telegram and Sun* Newspaper Photograph Collection
96. Gibson: Fred Palumbo, photographer, 1956, Library of Congress Prints and Photographs Division, *New York World-Telegram and Sun* Newspaper Photograph Collection
97. Dimaggio: Play Ball baseball cards, published by Bowman Gum, released into the Public Domain, copyright not renewed
98. Namath: *Jet Stream* magazine published 1965, published without copyright notice, entered into the Public Domain
99. Ashe: Rob/Anefo Bogaerts photograph, 1975, from the Dutch National Archives, Nationaal Archief Fotocollectie Anefo, licensed under the Creative Commons agreement
100. Jabbar: Frank Bryan, photographer, 1974, *The Sporting News* archives, published without copyright notice, entered into the Public Domain

ACKNOWLEDGMENTS

Every one of my teachers has been a great New Yorker and I so deeply thank each of them for turning me into a writer: Mrs. Bookman, Ms. Glembocki, Ms. Scott, Ms. Kirkpatrick, Ms. Stewart, Ms. Grant, Ms. Lau, Ms. Seitz, Mr. Schorr, Ms. Truss, Ms. Chambers, Ms. McGarrity, Ms. Freire, Mr. Dimino, Ms. C. Olsen, Mr. Sylvester, Ms. Regan, Mr. Ceci, Dr. Zizak, Ms. Varugheese, Ms. Custer, Ms. N. Olsen, Ms. Lodespoto, Ms. Molen, Mr. Rivera, Ms. Pawson, Ms. Nadel, Ms. Ng, Ms. Djaghrouri, Ms. Luca, Ms. Medina, Ms. Cullen, Ms. Jaffe and the great Ms. McGarr and Mr. Berman.

Thank you to my friends for their constant support: Brisa, Rusudan, Gabriella, all my PPYRC teammates and my friends at Christa McAuliffe Middle School. My cousins and aunts and uncles and grandparents all inspire me and I love them. I love my brother, Shaw, and thank him for his endless good humor. I thank my mom for her proofreading and my dad for his editing and guidance. Thanks, Mom and Dad!

Brooklyn Bridge Books Icon made by Freepik from www.flaticon.com

Lastly, this book would not exist without Steve Tiano. Steve is a freelance book designer and he took this project under his wing because he grew up near where we live and because he was reminded of when he first wrote a story and tried to make a book out of it. Steve led me to the finish and handled all the details. He made this book look better than my wildest dreams. Steve, you are greatest and I owe you!!!

INDEX

Abdul-Jabbar, Kareem, 134
Anthony, Susan B., 16
Ashe, Arthur, 133
Asimov, Isaac, 124
Astor, Brooke, 89
Austen, Alice, 101
Balanchine, George, 112
Baldwin, James, 110
Bloomberg, Michael, 40
Bly, Nellie, 117
Bourke-White, Margaret, 111
Brady, Mathew, 55
Breslin, Jimmy, 119
Chisholm, Shirley, 31
Cooper, Peter, 62
Corbin, Margaret, 37
Cuomo, Mario, 49
Da Verrazzano, Giovanni, 73
De Mille, Agnes, 99
DiMaggio, Joe, 131
Ellison, Ralph, 104
Ferraro, Geraldine, 36
Feynman, Richard, 84
Foo, Wong Chin, 17
Fulton, Robert, 76
Gaston, Rosetta "Mother," 19
Gayle, Margot, 53
Gershwin, George, 113
Gibson, Althea, 130
Ginsburg, Ruth Bader, 35
Giuliani, Rudy, 38
Goldman, Emma, 21
Gompers, Samue, 20
Graham, Martha, 106
Guggenheim, Peggy, 92
Hamilton, Alexander, 34
Henson, Jim, 102
Ho, David, 77
Holiday, Billie, 108
Hudson, Henry, 81
Hughes, Langston, 98
Hurston, Zora Neale, 118
Hutchinson, Anne, 39
Huxtable, Ada Louise, 120
Jacobs, Jane, 54
Jay, John, 32
Kissinger, Henry, 50
La Guardia, Fiorello, 33
Lebow, Fred, 68
Lombardi, Vince, 129

Lowell, Josephine Shaw, 26
Marx Brothers, 109
Mathews, Victoria Earle, 22
McKinney-Steward, Susan, 80
Mead, Margaret, 83
Minuit, Peter, 75
Moody, Lady Deborah, 43
Motley, Constance Baker, 41
Namath, Joe "Willie," 132
Olmstead, Frederick Law, 67
Onassis, Jacqueline Kennedy, 56
O'Neill, Eugene, 107
Oppenheimer, J. Robert, 74
Ovington, Mary White, 28
Pantoja, Antonia, 27
Papp, Joseph "Joe," 66
Parker, Dorothy, 122
Perkins, Francis, 48
Rand, Ayn, 123
Riis, Jacob, 25
Robinson, Jackie, 127
Rockefeller, Abby Aldrich, 91
Roebling, Emily & Washington, 64
Rohatyn, Felix, 42
Roosevelt, Eleanor, 45
Roosevelt, Franklin D., 44
Roosevelt, Theodore, 46
Ruth, George Herman "Babe," 128
Sagan, Carl, 82
Salk, Jonas, 79
Schiff, Dorothy, 61
Schneiderman, Rose, 24
Scorsese, Martin, 105
Seinfield, Jerry, 100
Seixas, Gershom Mendes, 23
Steinbrenner, George, 65
Stuyvesant, Peter, 78
Tappan, Lewis, 18
Tesla, Nikola, 85
Tiffany, Louis Comfort, 103
Toussaint, Pierre, 90
Trump, Donald J., 47
Vanderbilt, Cornelius, 69
Wald, Lillian, 15
Walker, Madam C.J., 63
Warhol, Andy, 97
White, Alfred T., 93
Whitman, Walt, 121
Wittenberg, Ruth, 57
Yellen, Janet, 86

ABOUT THE AUTHOR

Agatha Edwards began writing this book in the eighth grade. She attended P.S. 10 in Brooklyn from kindergarten through third grade, P.S. 230 in fourth and fifth grades, and the Christa McAuliffe Middle School in Brooklyn. She has participated in the Hunter College Summer Enrichment Program for the Gifted, was a member of the National Junior Honor Society, the Kiwanis Builders Club, the Christa McAuliffe Debate and Basketball Teams, and Girls Learn International (GLI). She studies piano at Brooklyn College and plays in the Kaufman Center's "Face the Music" Symphony in Manhattan. An avid runner, she is a member of the Prospect Park Youth Running Club and was part of their AAU All-American team in 2016. She is a student at Stuyvesant High School in New York City, class of 2021. Her previous books are fiction and include *Grace and Suzie, The Mystery in Arches* and *The Mystery in Badlands*. She lives with her parents and brother in Brooklyn, New York.

Comments, feedback, corrections?
Please write us at: The100mostimportant@gmail.com

This book is available at Amazon.com

For orders of 10 or more and bulk discounts, please write to:
Brooklynbridgebooks@gmail.com